Emerging Roles for Community College Leaders

Richard L. Alfred, Paul A. Elsner,
R. Jan LeCroy, Nancy Armes, *Editors*

NEW DIRECTIONS FOR COMMUNITY COLLEGES

Sponsored by the ERIC Clearinghouse for Junior Colleges

ARTHUR M. COHEN, *Editor-in Chief*
FLORENCE B. BRAWER, *Associate Editor*

Number 46, June 1984

Paperback sourcebooks in
The Jossey-Bass Higher Education Series

Jossey-Bass Inc., Publishers
San Francisco • Washington • London

EDUCATIONAL RESOURCES INFORMATION CENTER

Clearinghouse For Junior Colleges

UNIVERSITY OF CALIFORNIA, LOS ANGELES

Richard L. Alfred, Paul A. Elsner, R., Jan LeCroy, Nancy Armes (Eds.).
Emerging Roles for Community College Leaders.
New Directions for Community Colleges, no. 46.
Volume XII, number 2.
San Francisco: Jossey-Bass, 1984.

New Directions for Community Colleges Series
Arthur M. Cohen, *Editor-in-Chief*; Florence B. Brawer, *Associate Editor*

New Directions for Community Colleges (publication number USPS 121-710)
is published quarterly by Jossey-Bass Inc., Publishers, in association with
the ERIC Clearinghouse for Junior Colleges. *New Directions* is numbered
sequentially — please order extra copies by sequential number. The volume
and issue numbers above are included for the convenience of libraries.
Second-class postage rates paid at San Francisco, California, and at additional
mailing offices.

The material in this publication was prepared pursuant to a contract
with the National Institute of Education, U.S. Department of Education.
Contractors undertaking such projects under government sponsorship
are encouraged to express freely their judgment in professional and
technical matters. Prior to publication, the manuscript was submitted
to the Center for the Study of Community Colleges for critical review and
determination of professional competence. This publication has met such
standards. Points of view or opinions, however, do not necessarily represent
the official view or opinions of the Center for the Study of Community
Colleges or the National Institute of Education.

Correspondence:
Subscriptions, single-issue orders, change of address notices, undelivered
copies, and other correspondence should be sent to Subscriptions,
Jossey-Bass Inc., Publishers, 433 California Street, San Francisco
California 94104.

Editorial correspondence should be sent to the Editor-in-Chief,
Arthur M. Cohen, at the ERIC Clearinghouse for Junior Colleges,
University of California, Los Angeles, California 90024.

Library of Congress Catalogue Card Number LC 83-82720

International Standard Serial Number ISSN 0194-3081

International Standard Book Number ISBN 87589-988-9

Cover art by Willi Baum
Manufactured in the United States of America

This publication was prepared with funding from the National Institute of
Education, U.S. Department of Education, under contract no. 400-83-0030.
The opinions expressed in the report do not necessarily reflect the posi-
tions or policies of NIE or the Department.

Ordering Information

The paperback sourcebooks listed below are published quarterly and can be ordered either by subscription or single-copy.

Subscriptions cost $35.00 per year for institutions, agencies, and libraries. Individuals can subscribe at the special rate of $25.00 per year *if payment is by personal check.* (Note that the full rate of $35.00 applies if payment is by institutional check, even if the subscription is designated for an individual.) Standing orders are accepted. Subscriptions normally begin with the first of the four sourcebooks in the current publication year of the series. When ordering, please indicate if you prefer your subscription to begin with the first issue of the *coming* year.

Single copies are available at $8.95 when payment accompanies order, and *all single-copy orders under $25.00 must include payment.* (California, New Jersey, New York, and Washington, D.C., residents please include appropriate sales tax.) For billed orders, cost per copy is $8.95 plus postage and handling. (Prices subject to change without notice.)

Bulk orders (ten or more copies) of any individual sourcebook are available at the following discounted prices: 10–49 copies, $8.05 each; 50–100 copies, $7.15 each; over 100 copies, *inquire.* Sales tax and postage and handling charges apply as for single copy orders.

To ensure correct and prompt delivery, all orders must give either the *name of an individual* or an *official purchase order number.* Please submit your order as follows:

Subscriptions: specify series and year subscription is to begin.
Single Copies: specify sourcebook code (such as, CC8) and first two words of title.

Mail orders for United States and Possessions, Latin America, Canada, Japan, Australia, and New Zealand to:
Jossey-Bass Inc., Publishers
433 California Street
San Francisco, California 94104

Mail orders for all other parts of the world to:
Jossey-Bass Limited
28 Banner Street
London EC1Y 8QE

New Directions for Community Colleges Series
Arthur M. Cohen, *Editor-in-Chief*
Florence B. Brawer, *Associate Editor*

Contents

Leadership in community colleges cannot be conceptualized from a rational perspective. This chapter examines changing environmental conditions facing community colleges, and uses a symbolic interaction model to analyze the potential of administrators to provide leadership for institutional development.

Achievement of administrative priorities, particularly those that require organizational change, has become costly and complex. To achieve change in the coming decade, administrators will need more managerial sophistication to avoid such unacceptable costs as loss of organizational morale and managerial credibility.

Community colleges are forced to mold and select future leaders from the shaky, on-the-job crucible of politics, pressure groups, internal lineage, and word of mouth. This approach will not supply the farsighted, innovative thinking needed for an effective response to tomorrow's demands.

The role of the community college leader today is complex and multi-faceted. It involves the use of communications technology, considerable dependence on data for decision making, and working with a myriad of external organizations.

Editors' Notes

Community colleges are now in the midst of a transformation that may produce major and permanent changes in their mission, goals, and organizational structure. Central to this transformation is the role of leaders in recognizing the forces of change — advancing technology, public policy initiatives by government agencies, demographic transition, economic conditions, and societal attitudes — and in introducing reforms that adapt the college to the different dimensions of change. Change can be expected to have profound personal consequences for leaders and the individuals with whom they work. These consequences raise a number of questions. For example, what effects will the new technologies have on the delivery of instruction and on the conduct of administration? What repercussions will competition for students and staff from new educational providers have for community colleges with limited discretionary resources? What kinds of skills, knowledge, attitudes will leaders need to manage community colleges in the future? What are the characteristics of the leader who can adapt the institution to changing environmental conditions? What mix of academic training, experience, and socialization processes will prepare tomorrow's leaders to deal with the changes that face today's colleges? Will institutional needs for leaders competent in new managerial technologies exceed the supply available from traditional graduate programs and work-based leadership development programs?

This volume has an important purpose: to describe changes in the environment of leadership for community colleges that can improve methods for identifying and developing tomorrow's leaders. More than knowledge and understanding of change is required to provide leadership in complex organizations: Broad-based academic training, meaningful work experience, and important personality dimensions, such as flexibility and persistence, are also required. However, knowledge of the present context for leadership and of anticipated changes in economic, social, demographic and technological conditions is important for institutional efforts to locate — or develop from within — leaders who will guide the future development of community colleges.

The chapters in this volume are grouped into three sections. Each section focuses on a unique dimension of leadership. The first section describes the current context for leadership. In Chapter One, Richard L. Alfred presents a symbolic interaction model for analysis of leadership and depicts patterns of congruence and incongruence between the institution and its external environment that result from the quality of the institution's management and leadership. In Chapter Two, Richard C. Richardson, Jr., examines critical variables that will shape administrative behavior in the 1980s and outlines strategies that leaders can use to adapt community colleges to changing conditions. In Chapter Three, Paul A. Elsner focuses on strategies that can be used to develop future leaders and suggests responses that national and local government should implement to facilitate the preparation of leaders in the next decade.

The second section describes the dimensions of change in the external and internal environments for community college leadership. The first three chapters in this section address individual dimensions of change, while the last two chapters describe the skills needed to adapt the college to changing conditions. In Chapter Four, Robert H. McCabe presents a sociological overview of change in the role of community college president. New dimensions of institutional leadership are described, and examples of successful practices are provided to ensure that the reader understands the important concepts.

In Chapter Five, Joshua L. Smith examines the relationship between the college and the community and how changing demography, technology, manpower needs, and requirements for literacy affect the context for leadership. In Chapter Six, John N. Terrey considers the complex of economic and political developments that have caused college presidents to increase the time that they devote to external constituencies, such as the state legislature and business and industry. Noting that the community of community colleges is expanding, he advocates the formation of new alliances among business, government, and education to address problems related to economic development and recovery. In Chapter Seven, Ronald W. Bush and W. Clark Ames offer a futuristic perspective on the impact of changing technology on community college leaders. Bush and Ames focus special attention on the flexible staffing arrangements needed to adapt the institution to rapid technological change.

The third section addresses the question of how to identify and develop leaders for tomorrow's colleges. In Chapter Eight, Margaret MacTavish proposes an approach for selection of presidents that is based on a theory of leadership as contribution. In Chapter Nine, Judith S. Eaton provides insight into emerging forces in leadership, with particular attention to the role of women. In Chapter Ten, Thomas W. Fryer, Jr., considers the strengths and weaknesses of graduate education as preparation for leadership. Important and useful knowledge can be acquired through academic training, but it is questionable whether graduate programs are organized to provide such knowledge. Ten knowledge dimensions are proposed for study, and desirable qualities that may be susceptible to development through academic training are identified. In Chapter Eleven, R. Jan LeCroy argues the case for leadership development through work experience. The role of experience as teacher is described within the context of understudy, internship, and mentor relationships in the Dallas Community College District. Finally, in Chapter Twelve, Jim Palmer reviews the literature on two-year college presidents.

Clearly, educators and others make judgments about the quality of leadership. What criteria are used to judge quality? How good are today's leaders? Can the preparation of current and future leaders be improved? Where will we look for tomorrow's leaders? How should leaders be trained so that they can provide quality management in tomorrow's colleges? These questions are fundamental to the concept of leadership. Answers to these questions are basic for good internal management of community colleges. On the whole, these questions have been answered with lofty but vague rhetoric. Something more is now required, and community colleges are ill prepared to respond. The contributors to this volume examine the issue of leadership in community colleges. They point out the inherent complexities and ambiguities, and they outline the dimensions of change that tomorrow's leaders must understand if community colleges are to thrive in the coming decade.

Richard L. Alfred
Paul A. Elsner
R. Jan LeCroy
Nancy Armes

Richard L. Alfred is associate professor of higher education and director of the Community College Program at the University of Michigan, Ann Arbor.

Paul A. Elsner is chancellor, Maricopa County (Arizona) Community College District.

R. Jan LeCroy is chancellor of the Dallas County Community College District in Dallas, Texas.

Nancy Armes is special assistant to the president, Dallas County Community College District in Dallas, Texas.

PART 1.

The Context for Leadership Today

Leadership in community colleges cannot be conceptualized from a rational perspective. This chapter examines changing environmental conditions facing community colleges and uses a symbolic interaction model to analyze the potential of administrators to provide leadership for institutional development.

Maximizing Institutional Responsiveness to Changing Environmental Conditions

Richard L. Alfred

Leadership is a misunderstood but valued commodity in community college education today. Subject to the law of supply and demand, it is perhaps the single most important dimension linking institutional development with change in society's expectations and needs. There have always been questions concerning the quality of leadership. Not until recently, however, have the leadership capabilities of community college presidents, deans, and trustees been so rigorously and widely questioned. The fiscal stringency that affects most states, organized efforts to redefine the mission and purposes of higher education, and pressure to restructure the distribution of functions among institutions have made leadership a challenging but difficult task. This task can bring great satisfaction or deep depression, depending on the availability of success indicators and on the collective judgment of peers, subordinates, and valued constituencies.

The author thanks Gerlinda Melchiori, director of research and administration at the University of Michigan, for her assistance in designing and presenting the leadership concepts developed in this chapter.

R. L. Alfred, P. A. Elsner, R. J. LeCroy, N. Armes (Eds.). *Emerging Roles for Community College Leaders.*
New Directions for Community Colleges, no. 46. San Francisco: Jossey-Bass, June 1984.

This chapter examines changing environmental conditions facing community colleges and uses a symbolic interaction model to analyze the potential of administrators to provide leadership for institutional development. It examines the compatibility of leader and organizational behavior with emerging conditions, and it identifies problems in the capacity of presidents and chancellors to lead during a period of immense challenges for community colleges. The chapter concludes with a description of the qualities that tomorrow's leaders will need in order to manage institutions in transition.

Leadership: Yesterday and Today

As the identity of community colleges has changed, so have their operating needs and style of leadership. Almost from the beginning of the two-year college movement, presidents and chancellors emphasized a bureaucratic approach to leadership. Their organizational charts emphasized the vertical dimension, communication flowed along formal authority lines, and informal communication networks were discouraged if they hampered the advance of the institution toward important goals. To accommodate burgeoning enrollments, administrators needed skills in campus planning and construction, program design and development, staff recruitment, cost projections, and even leadership for the bond or special tax elections that were sometimes necessary in order to raise needed revenue. Questions were rarely raised about the quality of leadership, because resources were plentiful enough that mistakes and poor decisions could be tolerated. Organizational values gained through personal exposure to management in business and industry, government, and human service organizations led trustees to leave management to the president. In the resulting leadership climate, community college executives wielded considerable power. They became accustomed to autonomy in their decision making, and they enjoyed broad support in the development of programs and policies that met identified needs. Success was obvious as the number of students, courses, faculty, and programs increased.

With the advent of the 1980s, community colleges have felt the pressure of changing state and federal requirements guiding the allocation of resources, and the era of laissez faire leadership has ceased. Institutions increasingly depend on the state for their revenue. Now, they need elaborate plans detailing expected enrollment levels, program and staff expenditures, and capital needs in order to support their budget requests. In the past, the board and the college president shared responsibility for determining mission and establishing priorities and programs. Now, faculty unions, community interest groups, state agencies, and elected officials are demanding a stronger role in decision making. Community college leaders must be able to balance power among the coalitions that are coming to shape institutional decisions. Consider, for example, the complex network of interest groups that can coalesce to shape revenue and expenditure levels in the college budget: Outside the college, the state governor's office can target particular agencies for reduced or increased spending in a given budget year. The state budget office can publish fiscal guidelines outlining state economic conditions, financial priorities, and allowable costs that budget requests for the coming year must reflect. State legislators can sponsor legislation that directly or indirectly advances the interests of one segment of higher education over those of others in the appropriations process. Finally, coordinating boards can develop enrollment and resource allocation strategies that direct resources to particular institutions or programs in response to prevailing economic and demographic conditions. Within the college, faculty unions seeking to establish job protection language in collective bargaining agreements can drive up fixed costs. College deans and vice-presidents can seek to protect their units in future competition with other units for scarce resources by padding current requests for personnel and equipment, and academic departments can use the budget process to hedge against inflation or future austerity by enriching their equipment and supply inventories. Finally, trustees can push pet projects on behalf of special-interest groups in the community.

The perception that a community college presidency is no longer an attractive appointment is spreading. Indeed, the perception is now widespread among senior executives. Chief executive officers face controversies over the scope and definition of institutional mission, over the quality of academic degree and nondegree programs, over the mode of financing, and over the comparative advantages that favorable enrollment and tuition pricing policies have enabled community colleges to achieve.

Conceived of as a social innovation that placed postsecondary education within the reach of citizens who otherwise lacked the necessary economic and academic resources, two-year colleges have undergone an aging process similar to that which the four-year institutions experienced. There is considerable evidence of such aging on many fronts: deteriorating facilities, tenured faculty teaching outdated technical skills, students working with obsolete equipment, and legislation bearing on community colleges aimed at multiple agencies dependent on state support. Community colleges are no longer a unique component of postsecondary education. They are only one part of the total education delivery system.

Leadership in Symbolic Interaction Perspective

Community college administrators of yesterday and today share a tendency to view leadership as a gestalt involving process and entrepreneurial dimensions. From the entrepreneurial perspective, there are programs to develop, linkages to establish with external agencies, and staff to hire and train as needs dictate. The process side of leadership poses another agenda: Plans must be developed to focus and guide activity. Programs must be evaluated to determine their costs and benefits. Staff performance must be monitored, resources must be allocated, expenditures must be audited, and policies must be enforced. These leadership dimensions make at least four assumptions about the community college itself: First, a self-correcting rational system unites interdependent faculty and staff. Second, there is consensus on goals and the means of attaining them. Third, there is control through coordination of information dissemination to campus and extra-campus constituencies. Fourth, both the problems that an institution is likely to face and its solutions are predictable.

However, community colleges are not rational organizations. Consequently, the rational perspective that many administrators now hold is not useful. Much of the uniqueness of the individual public two-year college derives from the sharply defined geographic region that it serves. Administrators interact with multiple constituencies in this region and face an array of competing pressures that require a loosely knit organizational structure for successful performance. The indeterminate nature of the college's mission, goals, and academic degree programs constitutes direct evidence of the loosely knit structure developed over time to adapt the institution to its environment.

The loosely knit structure is sensitive to changing environmental conditions and to alterations in the balance of power among internal and external constituencies. The term *symbolic interaction* can be used to describe the complex of conditions and constituencies that interact to shape academic decisions and leader behavior. As Figure 1 shows, symbolic interaction portrays leadership as a catalyst that adapts the internal organization to changing environmental conditions, thereby producing congruence, or that retards change, thereby producing incongruence. Inept administrators can do much to constrain the leadership potential of executive office, and that potential can just as easily be limited by developments external to the institution. There are a number

Figure 1. Symbolic Interaction Model for Leadership

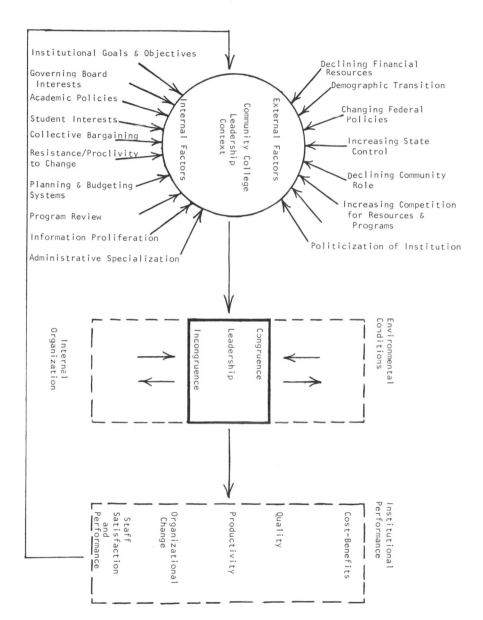

of external constraints: Demographic changes have meant fewer high school graduates. As a result, the college president must devote a significant amount of attention to enrollment planning, which serves to diminish the time available for academic decisions. Curtailment of economic growth has constricted the availability and flow of resources, since almost all money inside and outside the institution is committed. As a result, the president has less opportunity to reshape the institution by guiding the flow of resources. Moreover, competition for both students and financial resources is rising from elementary and secondary school systems and from public four-year colleges and universities. Thus, presidents and chancellors will need to identify strategies that can safeguard the mission and programs of community colleges from encroachment by school systems and four-year colleges seeking new markets by expanding their programs to include technical education and by broadening their recruitment strategies to include adult learners. The national community college movement is increasingly being fragmented into a state-by-state movement, and federal and state legislation aimed specifically at community colleges has changed as a result. Leaders will be challenged to identify the unique mission of the community college and to provide cogent arguments for state support. At the same time, social attitudes that are emerging among population groups — rejection of authority, intensification of criticism, increased skepticism — subject leadership in a growing number of community colleges to suspicion and doubt. Federal laws and regulations affecting college policies and procedures are increasing. As a result, presidents and boards of trustees do not possess total jurisdiction over institutional programs and services. Courts too are taking an increasing part in decisions that once were considered internal. Leaders have lost full control over decisions related to staff selection and retention, work conditions, and academic progression and retention standards. Line-item budgeting, centralized control of purchasing and personnel, and sophisticated information systems that make budget development and reporting a complex process have increased the control of state agencies over college budgets. Presidents can no longer generate and allocate resources according to personal judgment or that of faculty and staff. Increased investigative activity by local media often projects a negative image of the college to citizens in the service region. Community college leaders are increasingly being called on to defend the integrity of the college in such matters as student outcomes, financial transactions, curriculum design, and academic standards. Special-interest groups have intensified their efforts to affect decisions. Presidents and chancellors must selectively involve interest groups in decisions affecting the community. This dilutes the scope and extent of their own personal authority in the decision-making process. Finally, the recent "sunshine" laws and practices affect the privacy of a decision-making process and thereby alter the shape and effectiveness of management decisions.

One should not view these external influences on community college leadership as a short-term aberration associated with a declining economy. They depict a new reality for community colleges: The longer a community college is in operation, the less politically attractive it becomes. Consequently, public support for a developing institution with unique characteristics of open access and low tuition becomes public concern about an established organization with spiraling maintenance and labor costs. Maintenance funding is much less attractive politically than developmental funding. It allows productivity issues — for example, the rising cost of settlements reached through collective bargaining, enrollment and retention policies, and articulation practices — to take primacy over ideological issues — for example, mission, goals, and purposes — and it dramatically alters the turf for leadership.

Facing this altered turf, community college presidents and chancellors seem to feel that they must achieve control over the external environment. Such control seems impossible. Students have very different backgrounds and academic skills. Moreover, administrators have no firm standards by which to judge the impact of the institution and its programs on the constituencies that it serves, and they have no clear concept of causation that specifies the effects of the activities that they undertake. Further, these effects are indirect. In comparison with other public agencies, community colleges do not appear in the short term to be a good investment. In contrast, other human service organizations have developed manifest and direct indicators of the outcomes that they produce and of the effects of a shortfall in resources on their services. For example, sanitation departments can produce data showing the relation between refuse collection schedules and budget reductions. Law enforcement agencies can show that caseloads require officers to concentrate their efforts on the apprehension of felony suspects and neglect other types of criminal activity. Fire protection agencies can show that budget reductions force fire stations to be closed and response time to increase. Hospitals and health organizations can relate budget reductions to a decline in the number of beds available for specific categories of patients. Courts can show that budget cuts can cause the prosecution of specific types of criminal activity to be curtailed or eliminated. Community colleges stand at a disadvantage in cost-benefit comparisons with other human service organizations. Will community college presidents and chancellors be able to provide the type of leadership needed to counterbalance or negate this disadvantage in the coming years?

The influence of the presidency can also be altered by internal developments. A number of forces are at work. Faculty control over appointments, promotions, and academic policy has increased over the years. Presidents and chancellors can exercise control over curriculum by encouraging or discouraging faculty initiatives and through the budgets that they present to trustees for adoption. However, they often fail to exercise their authority and power to the fullest extent in academic policy matters, since they often fail to address complex questions involving curriculum structure, degree requirements, and academic standards directly. As a result, control over such matters devolves to faculty. Increasing numbers of faculty members are joining unions, and the provisions of the contract are replacing more individually made decisions. In many institutions, boards are assuming increased responsibility for decision making and no longer restricting themselves to policy formation alone. Students too are taking a greater part in decision making. Increasingly, students are being represented by special-interest groups, such as part-time students, financial aid recipients, returning adult learners, and displaced workers. Thus, decision making focuses on individual goals and less on institutional goals. The doctrine of participatory governance increases the consultation and attention that the executive devotes to any one initiative, but the cost is less action, because each group has the power of veto. The increasing size and complexity of community colleges has led to elaborate systems for communication and decision making. Presidents and chancellors can no longer employ personal authority in decision making, and in many cases they must depend on reports and memoranda generated by individuals one or two levels below them. The increasing sophistication and complexity of the information available to support decisions increases the difficulty of decision making and encourages administrators to emphasize the procedures used to make a decision over the outcomes produced by the decision. Finally, with the increasing specialization of administrative staff, many administrators lack experience in institution-wide management, and they cannot bring multiple perspectives to the decision process.

As conditions change and as administrators seek new ways of adapting the institution to its environment, problems begin to emerge with respect to control over parties to the decision-making process. Administrators are frustrated as coordinating boards, faculty, legislators, state budget officers, and citizen groups gain in influence. They are frustrated because they expend much energy to reach worthwhile goals, but their actual accomplishments fail to adapt the institution to its environment, thereby producing incongruence. Incongruence allows faculty and staff to perceive the need for structural change. More often than not, the focal point of this change process is the chief executive officer, who must separate from the institution to facilitate the achievement of goals more in keeping with emerging conditions. Presidents and chancellors who lack organizational consciousness, who cannot discern changes in the environment, who lack true cost-consciousness, and who avoid difficult decisions because the risks are too great will find community college leadership an increasingly burdensome task in the difficult period that lies ahead.

Leadership in Crisis?

Viewing leadership as a function of the match between individual, institution, and environment, one is led to ask, Is community college leadership in crisis? The answer is that the position of chief executive officer is in crisis. The crisis centers not on the skills of the individuals who occupy that position but on the requisites of the position itself. Conversations with presidents and chancellors, top academic officers, professional search personnel, and ex-presidents indicate that the image of the college presidency has deteriorated (Kerr and others, 1983). The management of decline is not attractive, and participatory democracy makes it very hard to make timely and meaningful decisions after exhaustive consultation. Modern life-styles do not make long hours of work attractive, and the wide range of contacts determined by the job makes privacy a scarce but valued commodity. The presidency has become an almost exclusively external job, as the emphasis on fund raising and on public relations has increased and as contact with faculty, students, and academic issues has decreased.

Community college presidents experience great difficulty and discomfort when the board of trustees departs from policy making and intrudes into management. Where the president inherits a staff, he or she often cannot make changes because of "untouchables" protected by the board or by important board members. The presence of untouchables reflects friendships formed over time, favors exchanged, the desire of board members to have their own independent channels of information, and respect or admiration for past performance. Where the turnover of presidents has been rapid, boards can come to depend on second-level officers, who sustain day-to-day operations and assure continuity. All these developments have had an adverse impact on the presidency — they erode the power of the position and create a crisis in leadership (Kerr and others, 1983).

Finally, as external pressures command increasingly large shares of the president's time and attention, the problems of specialization and presidential detachment from academic decision making have increased. Faculty have de facto control over most decisions related to courses, programs, and academic standards. Consequently, community college presidents have moved to split the executive management into an "outside" dimension and an "inside" dimension with the president reporting to the board and the vice-president or dean to the faculty. Specialization of administrative functions at the midmanagement level further removes the president from the complexities of internal decision making. There is a relatively large administrative support staff and many constituencies to serve inside and outside the college. Since outcome measures are ambiguous, presidents implement elaborate administrative processes to coordinate the efforts of staff to reach identified goals. Long-range planning has become a popular strategy for introducing control over rapidly changing external conditions. Program review has gained acceptance as a method for justifying difficult decisions about resources, and reallocation is attracting increasing interest as a method for locating revenue that can be used to develop new programs and services.

Every time another specialist is inserted between the president and lower levels of management, the president's control over faculty and staff is loosened. As a result, community college leaders need group management skills similar to those that the executive officers of other complex social organizations possess. This need is evident in at least three recent developments in community college management: First, at many schools a presidential cabinet of senior administrators meets regularly — at least weekly in most cases — with the chief executive to discuss a wide range of college issues. Second, a high-ranking academic officer — provost, academic vice-president, or dean of faculty with the status of vice-president — is typically acknowledged as second in command or at the very least as primus inter pares by fellow cabinet officers. Third, the president must balance the scheduling of his or her time with his or her own predilection for dealing personally with academic policy decisions (Kerr and others, 1983).

When we examine the distribution of time in the executive work week, the concrete activities that dominate the president's work load, and the areas for which policy must be enacted, we see that community college leaders are overburdened with "people-meeting" and resource development functions that make it difficult for them to develop an appreciation of the institution's internal dynamics. Their management skills face seemingly irreconcilable demands. For example, they must be able to strike a balance between competing demands for cooperation or competition with providers of postsecondary education, immediate or delayed response with special-interest groups, variable or common core academic programs for students with diverse academic backgrounds, and organizational stability to handle present demands or organizational change to address future needs with internal and external constituencies. The time that administrators spend on addressing these demands is often treated — mistakenly — as evidence of indecisiveness and ineffective leadership. This judgment results from application of a rational model to leadership. When presidents do not measure up to the standards of that model, scapegoats are sought. Administrators acquiesce in this line of reasoning when they accept rational standards as the measure of their leadership skills. They seldom realize that leadership cannot be measured solely in terms of rational indicators. Leadership is a product of opportunity, training, initiative, and instincts that creatively adapt an institution to its environment.

Leaders for Tomorrow

Effective leaders in tomorrow's community colleges will not be heroic individuals with multiple skills and charismatic personal qualities. They will enter administrative positions on the basis of interest and early success in complex organizations, and the amount of time that they spend in any one position will be determined by an acute sense of when it is time to move on to the next position. Tomorrow's leaders will combine a conceptual understanding of the dynamics of complex organizations with meaningful and broad-ranging experience — often through direct contact with strong role models. They will be able to forge associations between complex events, such as teaching and learning, costs and benefits, plans and achievements, and programs and quality. Most important, they will realize that there is no formula for training the effective leader. Instincts are often as important as experience and formal training.

Administrative leadership to serve the future needs of community colleges can be cultivated and evaluated. The stages and components of leadership development described by Birnbaum (1983) can be useful in forming it. The stages in leadership development are sequential. Each stage involves specific skills and orientations, which can be learned. The components represent elements of training, experience, and exposure that facilitate the development of desirable leader characteristics. There are four stages of leadership development: internalization of appropriate decision behavior, effective performance of operational management functions, capacity to delegate authority and manage the total organizational environment, and capacity to diagnose requisites for change and provide leadership for organizational development. There are eight components of leadership development: socialization experience in complex organizations prior to career entry, academic training, nonacademic experience, academic experience, exposure to role models and talented peers, access to new ideas, exposure to challenging problems, and integration of ideas, experience, training, and instincts.

According to Birnbaum (1983), the critical element in the first stage of leadership development is preparation that can make potential leaders able to avert poor decisions and make good ones. They need a thorough understanding of the academic organization, administrative procedures, faculty values, and the interests and concerns of those whom they will lead. In the second stage, developing leaders learn to administer operational management processes in a manner seen as efficient, effective, and prudent by colleagues and constituencies. Knowledgeable of the need not to violate important academic norms, they must operate the institution's support activities in ways that remove nagging administrative problems from those who must devote their efforts to teaching. The third stage is predicated on the proposition that leaders cannot introduce and promote change personally. To make needed changes, the effective leader must delegate authority to subordinates and colleagues and minimize the constraints that inhibit their productivity. In the fourth stage, leaders learn to lead the change process. In the next decade, community colleges will enter a period of challenge and assessment in which programs, degree structures, academic standards, and basic values will be questioned both inside and outside the institution. During this time, every leader will encounter pressures to change the institutional structure and purposes reflected in the mission statement. Effective leaders will accurately gauge the nature of external conditions, sense the opportunity to secure a planned program of change, and propose a change process that is seen by faculty and staff as a way of resolving uncertainties and pursuing new agendas for development.

To reach the final stage of development, community college leaders will need to understand behavioral science concepts and their application to organizational change and development. Leadership preparation accomplished through merger of experience and academic training will provide valuable insights into the relationship between theory and action. The effective leader will be able to integrate diverse facets of academic training, academic and nonacademic experience, human relationships, and instincts to gauge the direction and intensity of changing conditions and recognize the potential in situations for organizational change. The nonleader who occupies a senior administrative position is likely to use a single dimension to make decisions that maintain the current shape of the organization and that fail to adapt to changing conditions.

ing from concrete, practical experience in administration to academic preparation at the graduate and undergraduate levels. Socialization experience in different types of organizations is integral to the development of capable leaders. This experience will be both educational and experiential in nature; it is essential for understanding the value systems of the community college as a complex organization.

Socialization experience is of little value to emerging leaders if relationships with peers and role models do not expose them to challenging problems and new ideas. The young professional must develop good management habits. This can best be accomplished through exposure to mentors who possess the wisdom of years of experience. Peers and subordinates play an important role in the development of leaders, because they provide immediate feedback about the effectiveness of decisions and administrative behavior in day-to-day situations. To a considerable extent, leaders are a product of the quality of the individuals with whom they work. Low-quality professionals breed poor work habits, while high-quality professionals engender work habits that are essential for good management.

Tomorrow's leaders will be those who can integrate diverse components of development — education, experience, and relationships with peers and role models — into a meaningful whole. They will be able to build a management infrastructure that can effectively interpret the mission and role of the institution within the regional educational delivery system, maintain balance and perspective in setting institutional priorities and managing scarce resources, and encourage vision beyond immediate social and economic conditions toward the goal of excellence in programs and services.

References

Birnbaum, R. "Searching for a Leader." *AAHE Bulletin,* 1983, *35* (9), 9–11.
Kerr, C., and others. *Strengthening Presidential Leadership in Colleges and Universities.* Unpublished report presented to the Association for Governing Boards, New York, September 1983.

Richard L. Alfred is associate professor of higher education and director of the Community College Program at the University of Michigan.

*Achievement of administrative priorities, particularly those
that require organizational change, has become costly and
complex. To achieve change in the coming decade,
administrators will need managerial sophistication to
avoid such unacceptable costs as loss of organizational
morale and managerial credibility.*

Management Challenges,
Principles, and Strategies
for the 1980s

Richard C. Richardson, Jr.

No crystal ball is needed to identify the critical variables that will shape
administrative behavior in the 1980s. Internal and external constraints
to effective leadership have become increasingly clear as the watershed
of the seventies recedes with the passage of time. This chapter reviews
the forces that influence leadership and suggest directions that will
enable community college administrators to respond to new challenges.

Forces Influencing Community College Leadership

Demographic Influences. The end of the baby boom means that
the number of students of traditional age will decline through 1984.
The effects of this overall decline of 26 percent will be differentiated.
Some states will experience cohort declines in excess of 40 percent,
while other states will experience modest growth (Breneman, 1982). In
general, the states that will experience the greatest declines are those
with the largest number of colleges and the highest percentage of
private institutions. Competition will be intense for students of tradi-

R. L. Alfred, P. A. Elsner, R. J. LeCroy, N. Armes (Eds.). *Emerging Roles for Community College Leaders.*
New Directions for Community Colleges, no. 46. San Francisco: Jossey-Bass, June 1984.

tional college age. Both the states and the federal government are likely to seek ways of equalizing costs for students in private institutions by providing subsidies of the type recently enacted by the Ohio state legislature.

The composition of the age groups that remain will also change. The percentages of blacks and Hispanics, groups that currently persist at much lower rates than the general college population, will increase. Four-year colleges and universities will be placed under growing pressure to assume their fair share of responsibility for these groups. They will respond by recruiting those with the best credentials, leaving the task of serving the most deficient to the community colleges.

The effects of these changing demographics are already evident in most community colleges, but they are likely to intensify in the future. Growing numbers of adults with family and job responsibilities seek courses that have an immediate economic return. Program integrity is threatened by the need of institutions to enroll large numbers of students in entry-level courses in order to maintain their budget base. High percentages of students who have no interest in earning an associate degree encourage the neglect of sequential course scheduling and academic advising. Students interested in pursuing a degree or in completing a work-specific program find it less costly in time to attend a four-year college or a proprietary technical institute. The transfer function is threatened, and the small number of community college graduates raises questions in the public mind about institutional productivity and effectiveness.

Finally, there is growing debate about who should serve the substantial segment of the population who are unemployed and who have never graduated from high school. Retraining is not the answer for those who possess marginal skills. This population has been a target for community college rhetoric and recruiting efforts, but there is little agreement about what could or should be done for its members, and the data on the effects of community college efforts to serve them are limited.

Resource Constraints. Most states have faced serious fiscal pressure at one time or another within the past five years. Even the energy-rich states have experienced economic dislocations as a result of the oil glut. There is fierce competition for the state dollars that are appropriated. Achievement of administrative priorities, particularly those that require organizational change, has become more costly and complex. Change can no longer be achieved by addition. Sometimes, it is not change that causes conflict but a choice of what is to be maintained, as exemplified in the decision of one community college district to preserve instructional television at the expense of faculty jobs. To achieve change in the coming decade, administrators will need managerial sophistication in order to avoid such unacceptable costs as loss of organizational morale and managerial credibility.

Mission Definition and Quality Assurance. The demographics of the changing student population, enrollment-driven funding formulas, and a philosophic commitment to serve a broad segment of the population have caused the mission of community colleges to expand. In the past, that expansion was limited only by the interests of those attending and by the resources available. To enhance eligibility for state dollars, it became common practice to describe curriculum offerings in terms that made courses compatible with the provisions in state funding formulas that provided the most reimbursement. Considerable technical expertise developed in justifying the inclusion of courses in career programs that were little more than a recombination of existing underenrolled courses. Such programs were designed more for marketing purposes than for teaching employable skills.

In the interests of maximizing the flow of state funds, community college leaders have been more than willing to leave the determination of what is transferable to the universities and of what is career-oriented to the state coordinating agencies. While this strategy has worked within limits, the practice of continuing to expand course offerings and mission definition even as resources were constrained has led to concerns about quality. Four-year colleges and universities, partly in self-defense, have developed the practice of assigning elective credit to courses that they question. This seems to increase the time that transfers must spend to earn a degree, because they have too many elective hours and too few required courses. Universities have also sought to impose requirements for transfers not applicable to native students moving from sophomore to junior status, such as higher grade point averages and achievement test scores. State agencies have been more direct in their response to community college expansion by capping enrollment, instituting penalties for overenrollment, and setting ceilings on reimbursement regardless of the number of students enrolled.

Technological Change and Aging Staff. Changes in the external environment, particularly changes in technology, have had considerable impact on aging administrators and faculty. While individuals are receptive to change, they have to be motivated, and few faculty are as fascinated with change as senior administrators, who see causing change as their principal raison d'être. Working with faculty committed to performing services for which there is no longer adequate demand may be the single most difficult challenge that administrators will face in the next ten years. At the same time, pressure from new influence groups, such as women and minorities, for a greater share of policy positions creates problems within the ranks of administrators. Concurrently, the options of those already in administrative positions are shrinking, competition has increased for a declining number of opportunities. Keeping those who are not promoted in the trenches as effective contributors will constitute a challenge second only to the problem of renewing faculty.

There is also the problem of maintaining perspective in dealing with issues involving the use of technology in classrooms and administrative offices. Discussions will come to center on such questions as, When do the costs of employing technology exceed the marginal increases in effectiveness or efficiency? and What forms of human interaction are indispensable in the service organization? The decision to implement technology should be based on consideration of its costs and benefits.

Leading Community Colleges in the 1980s

To deal with the issues just reviewed, administrators will require skills different from the ones needed to start new institutions or greatly expand existing ones in the sixties and early seventies. The problems now emerging call more for developing staff than for building campuses. The external environment can no longer be viewed as a source of support that can keep pace with rising enrollments. Administrators will be held accountable for the decisions that they make and for the outcomes of these decisions. Boards have become intrusive in day-to-day management, as external and internal environments have become less predictable. As local and state-level boards try out new roles, administrators experience less flexibility in their own sphere of decision making, and the distinctions between setting policy and administering the institutions become blurred.

Changing Principles for Leadership. Concurrent with the issues raised by the changing climate for governance are knotty problems related to administrative practice, such as organizational redesign, assessment of organizational effectiveness, faculty and administrative commitment to organizational priorities, and professional renewal for staff and administrators. A welter of conflicting theories and advice about how to improve administrative practice has been advanced in recent years. One work stands out, because it provides usable information about management practices in America's best-run corporations while integrating much of what can be gleaned from a variety of organizational studies conducted over the past fifty years (Peters and Waterman, 1982). These authors describe eight characteristics that differentiate excellent corporations from less effective counterparts. I have rewritten their descriptions so as to make them applicable to community colleges. I have used question form, so that the descriptions can be used to assess current management practices.

First, can the college administration address problems and implement solutions within a reasonable period of time? Is the committee structure manageable? Are there built-in deadlines by which responsibility passes to the next highest echelon regardless of action or inaction? Do administrators consistently achieve a reasonable balance between informed solutions and timely action?

Second, does the institution take pride in providing reliable services of high quality to its clients? Do faculty and administrators listen regularly and intently to what clients say in surveys and interviews or what they hear when they are just walking around? Listening to clients is not the same thing as listening to advisory committees, who may or may not be clients.

Third, do senior administrators regularly encourage practical risk taking and good trics among faculty, junior administrators, and other staff members? Do highly placed administrators, as a matter of policy, make a reasonable number of mistakes? According to Peters and Waterman, answering no to these questions suggests insufficient levels of autonomy and entrepreneurship among executive managers.

Fourth, do administrators emphasize the role of faculty and other staff members as the source of gains in quality and productivity? Do they avoid encouraging we/they attitudes in labor relationships and contracts? Does top administration exhibit respect for all faculty members and see them as a source of ideas as well as of fifteen credit hours of instruction?

Fifth, does top administration place its greatest emphasis on the philosophic commitments and central values of the institution, such as respect for students or the importance of learning, or is its primary concern with technological or economic resources, organizational structure, innovation, or timing?

Sixth, does the college confine its programming to areas in which it has appropriate expertise? Does the college offer programs that depend on external agents for the design of curriculum, assessment of relevance, and control of quality?

Seventh, is top administration characterized by simplicity and leanness? Peters and Waterman (1982) indicate that none of the corporations that they studied used a matrix structure for administration and that the few who had tried the structure dropped it after a period of experimentation.

Eighth, do administrators delegate responsibility and requisite authority to the operating levels of the organization, including individual instructors and task groups established to solve problems? Is there simultaneously a well-expressed and zealously defended set of core values for the institution from which solutions are derived?

The questions in this inventory are rooted deeply in what we know about human motivation but do not always practice. Positive reinforcement is more effective than negative sanctions. Institutional policies and procedures should permit staff to think of themselves as achievers. Individuals rely more on intuitive reasoning based on experience than on rational behavior based on the study of available data. While administrators value their own intuition, they less frequently give appropriate credit to the intuition of those with whom they work. Actions speak louder than words, and administrative behavior is a more powerful influence on faculty than the annual state-of-the-college address. Faculty and staff respond to external rewards and sanctions, but they also are driven by internal motivation. Each professional needs to feel a sense of purpose in what he or she is doing within the context of the organization (Peters and Waterman, 1982).

Administrators who think carefully about these points—most of which are obvious—will find ways of altering their behavior to make it more consistent with the leadership demands of the current decade. For example, the most obvious way for instructional administrators to encourage good teaching is to provide appropriate role models through their own teaching activities. One alternative is to spend at least as much time on identifying and recognizing good teachers as on evaluating and upgrading the inept. Clearly, there is a place for externally administered rewards and sanctions, but the process for accomplishing this must recognize internal needs and desires to do a good job, and it must allow most faculty and staff to emerge as achievers. Some methods must be found to enhance faculty and staff feelings about their own autonomy and the respect that the institution holds for them as individuals. A system of committees or an administrative structure that leads to organizational paralysis are not the answer.

Restructuring the Organization. Most discussions of community colleges as organizations are restricted to such issues as specialization by function or discipline, the relative advantages of centralization and decentralization, and alternative arrangements for involving faculty or students in decision making. Very little effort has been made to analyze the strengths and weaknesses of particular organizational forms under specific internal and external constraints. This approach has been greatly aided by the work of Mintzberg (1979), on whom the discussion that follows draws heavily.

In the 1960s and early 1970s, most community colleges used a form of organization that Mintzberg terms *simple structure,* because the colleges were both formative and small. Simple structure tends to centralize decision-making power in the hands of the chief executive. Because it is centralized, decision making is flexible and occurs without unnecessary delay. The process of formulating strategies is largely intuitive and nonanalytical, and it is entrepreneurial in its search for opportunities.

Despite its obvious virtues, the simple structure has fallen out of fashion, largely because its greatest strength, flexibility, is also its greatest weakness when growth and a changing environment dictate the need for more complex organizational responses. Centralization of decision-making authority allowed many chief executives to resist necessary change with great effectiveness. For many community colleges, movement away from the simple structure, which is increasingly being perceived by faculty as highly restrictive, occurred only with the departure, voluntary or otherwise, of the chief executives who either founded colleges or presided over their period of greatest growth.

The transition from simple structure, which is now largely complete in all but the smallest and most isolated community colleges, was accompanied by pervasive tensions over the future shape of the organization. Faculty oriented to clients and their professional specializations made clear their preference for professional bureaucracy, a form of organization that characterizes universities, hospitals, and related organizations that employ large numbers of professionals. Motivated by their close association with a complex and dynamic environment, administrators tended to prefer the administrative adhocracy — a type of organization ideally suited for pursuing the important objective of innovation. Because community colleges have been and continue to be dominated by administrators, they tend to display characteristics of the adhocracy. At the same time, faculty influence, which is increasingly being exercised through collective bargaining, places continuing pressure on administrators to incorporate characteristics of the professional bureaucracy. Currently, faculty are aided in this effort by changes in the external environment, which have increased the value of the professional bureaucracy, which promotes quality and efficiency by standardizing outputs, while simultaneously devaluing one of the principal strengths of the adhocracy, the ability to innovate and develop new products. Before discussing the implications of the alter-

natives that currently confront administrators for organizational structure, I will summarize Mintzberg's (1979) discussion of the characteristics of these two competing organizational forms.

The professional bureaucracy responds to two of the most
important contemporary needs of professionals: It delegates power to
them for their expertise, and it provides autonomy from the need to
coordinate closely with colleagues. Not only do professionals control
their own work, but they also seek to influence decisions important to
them — for example, those involving the distribution of resources and
the hiring and promotion of colleagues — by staffing administrative
positions from among their own number. Standardization of outputs
through enforcement of professional norms provides clients with
reasonable guarantees of the quality and uniformity of the services that
they receive. However, this advantage is accompanied by some liabil-
ities. There is little if any control over work by individuals outside the
profession, and there is no easy way of correcting problems involving
discretion or innovation. Incompetent or unconscientious professionals
can survive for long periods of time, and this reduces the effectiveness
of the organization.

In contrast, for the administrative adhocracy, problem solving
and innovation relies on identified support staff to carry out strategies
that emerge from decisions made over time. Adhocracies are tents
rather than palaces, and internal changes are frequent. Organizational
charts may be either unavailable or out of date. Faculty are cut off from
the main action or the cutting edge, because the responsibility for program development lies with support staff or temporary employees.
Adhocracies are the least stable form of organization, and they are
drawn toward bureaucratization as they age. This movement is
welcomed by staff, because it holds out the promise of stability and per-
mits faculty to concentrate on what they do best. At the same time,
evolutionary movements toward bureaucracy pose the threat that the
organization will lose its ability to innovate and hence to be competitive
in a dynamic environment. Adhocracies are not efficient at doing ordinary things, and this weakness creates pressure for change in the current environment for community college leadership.

Administrators can influence the process by which community
colleges reshape themselves. As our colleges advance toward the 1990s,
it seems increasingly clear that there is no single best organizational
form or approach to leadership. Determining the most productive form
for a specific institution requires several factors to be considered, including environmental constraints, internal preferences, and organizational priorities. All these factors are subject to change over time. In

the current setting, both employee organizations and sheer size seem to militate against the possibility of a return to simple structure. A second alternative involves accommodation of the pressures that are pushing community colleges toward becoming professional bureaucracies. It has the merit of responding to concerns about mission clarification and quality by reducing the scope of activities to those that faculty and staff are well prepared to carry out effectively. It would also help to reduce tensions between administrators and faculty, because administrators would come increasingly to share the values and perspectives of faculty. In many ways, this is an attractive scenario, but it has one serious flaw: By embracing the norms of the professional bureaucracy, the community college may purchase stability and harmony at the expense of its ability to respond quickly to changes in the external environment — its primary stock-in-trade for more than two decades. If not enough clients are interested in what current faculty do well, community colleges could lose the competitive edge that has helped them to offset losses among traditional students by attracting new clientele.

A third alternative involves continuing pursuit of administrative priorities through the adhocracy. While this seems to be the most likely course of action, since it involves little change from current practice, the likely consequences of retaining this form of organization are worth noting. First, valid questions can be raised about the need and capacity of an institution for rapid change when resources are scarce and when external constituents are more interested in improvements in the quality of existing services than in new services. Second, as Mintzberg (1979) makes clear, professionals who lose control over their own work become passive. Recent studies at Arizona State University (Richardson and others, 1983) identify the lack of faculty commitment to administrative priorities as a major contemporary problem in community colleges. Finally, since adhocracies are not efficient in performing ordinary tasks, the issue of cost-effectiveness creates a problem as public concern about accountability increases.

A fourth alternative is emerging in community college districts where a nontraditional "college without walls" has been created to serve as a center for innovation in the delivery of programs and services. These districts also operate one or more traditional campuses, primarily as professional bureaucracies, where faculty values generally prevail. The intent is to realize the advantages of adhocracy for innovation and quick response while using the strengths of professional bureaucracy to improve quality and reengage faculty and staff. It is still too early to evaluate the success of these efforts to achieve the best of both possible worlds. Districts that use this structure appear to operate in a state of dynamic tension, and there is conflict between the traditional colleges and the new colleges without walls on selected issues. On the surface, such conflicts seem to be at least as manageable as conflict in adhocracies, where less effort has been made to accommodate the values of professional staff.

Assessing and Achieving Organizational Effectiveness

While it is tempting to discuss changes in community college leadership behavior or organizational forms as if they represented places that administrators can move as they please, the fact is that the alternatives cannot be evaluated unless we attend to the results that they are expected to achieve. The general objective of administrative difficulty now is to assess organizational effectiveness in a way that will produce consensus about its presence or absence.

Recent efforts to deal with this complex variable have produced a number of promising results. Pfeffer and Salancik (1978) have constructed a resource-dependent classification of institutions. Under this classification, institutions must provide outcomes that are satisfactory to those who pay their bills. Where there are differences between the administrators who determine priorities and the external constituents who control resources, the choice is to change either the institution's priorities or the constituents' minds. In this view, organizational effectiveness is a measure of the degree to which the priorities of institutional managers and the preferences of external constituents coincide. The methodology suggested by this definition has been tested in Arizona in a study of two community colleges and their key external constituents (Richardson and others, 1982). The results have provided useful information to administrators and board members about the need to base definitions of institutional mission, organizational structure, and leadership strategies on empirical data and constituent perceptions, not on the subjective judgments of administrators and support staff.

In the 1980s, community college leaders will need to identify appropriate organizational and administrative outcomes before they address any of the other issues raised in this chapter. The first step is to define the outcomes that will establish an appropriate level of organizational effectiveness if they can be achieved. Next, these outcomes must be related to target constituencies. Where conflicts occur among the preferences of different constituents, some system of prioritization will have to be used to determine the preferences that should prevail. The values of those who provide the resources are likely to receive heavy weight. Once the outcomes have been prioritized, institutional research must establish baseline data about the extent to which high-priority outcomes are already being achieved. Community colleges have been notoriously lax in collecting such data. Evidence for at least some of the important outcomes will be difficult to obtain, but neither the difficulty involved in obtaining it nor the political sensitivity of the results should serve to deter leaders from the effort. The absence of data is bound to provoke estimates by external agencies that are more damaging than the actual data.

When a community college has identified its preferred outcomes and assessed the extent to which they are being achieved, it is in a position to define changes in leadership behavior and organizational form that must be made in order to improve performance. In the final analysis, presidents and chancellors will be able to identify effective leadership practices and improvements in organizational form only as they accumulate evidence that such practices or improvements have in fact made a difference in the effectiveness of their organization.

References

Breneman, D. W. *The Coming Enrollment Crisis: What Every Trustee Must Know.* Washington, D.C.: Association of Governing Boards of Colleges and Universities, 1982.

Mintzberg, H. *The Structuring of Organizations.* Englewood Cliffs, N.J.: Prentice-Hall, 1979.

Peters, T. J., and Waterman, R. H., Jr. *In Search of Excellence.* New York: Harper & Row, 1982.

Pfeffer, J., and Salancik, G. R. *The External Control of Organizations: A Resource-Dependence Perspective.* New York: Harper & Row, 1978.

Richardson, R. C., Jr., Doucette, D. S., and Armenta, R. *Missions of Arizona Community Colleges: A Research Description.* Tempe: Arizona State University, 1982. (ED 215 716)

Richardson, R. C., Jr., Fisk, E., and Okun, M. *Literacy in the Open-Access College.* San Francisco: Jossey-Bass, 1983.

Richard C. Richardson, Jr., is professor of higher education at Arizona State University in Temple, Arizona.

*Community colleges are forced to mold and select future
leaders from the shaky, on-the-job crucible of politics,
pressure groups, internal lineage, and word of mouth.
This approach will not supply the farsighted, innovative
thinking needed for an effective response to tomorrow's
demands.*

Meeting the Challenges
with New Leadership
Development Programs

Paul A. Elsner

The American community college movement has thus far declined to
make a critical investment in its future. We have avoided the arduous
undertaking of defining and characterizing the type of leadership that
we will need for the twenty-first century. Lacking a carefully designed
training paradigm, we are forced to mold and select our future leaders
from the shaky, on-the-job crucible of politics, pressure groups, internal lineage, and word of mouth. This approach will not supply the farsighted, innovative thinking needed for an effective community college
response to tomorrow's demands.

Not since the Kellogg Foundation funded junior college centers
in the 1960s has there been a systematic effort to train a national cadre
of leaders. The visibility and prominence now enjoyed by former
Kellogg fellows provides powerful testimony on the need to maintain a
continuous leadership pipeline. Other than a few notable efforts such
as the Leaders in the Eighties Project sponsored by the Fund for the
Improvement of Postsecondary Education and the American Council
on Education's National Identification Project, no organized, pervasive

R. L. Alfred, P. A. Elsner, R. J. LeCroy, N. Armes (Eds.). *Emerging Roles for Community College Leaders.*
New Directions for Community Colleges, no. 46. San Francisco: Jossey-Bass, June 1984.

leadership development process has been established. The results of this oversight may only be noticed slowly, as retirements cause the character of community college leadership gradually to change. Moreover, current practices in management and staff development will inexorably create a vacuum at the top.

This chapter addresses the need for future leadership in the community college movement. It explores some assumptions about the nature of leadership, change, and the future with a view toward identifying realistic organizational activities that leaders can undertake. It concludes by outlining some anticipatory strategies that can be used to develop leaders for tomorrow at both the local and the national level.

Leadership and Change

First Assumption: Organzations Do Change. March (1980, p. 1) replied to those who believe that many institutions are permanently stagnant: "Organizations change. They grow; they decline. They prosper; they fail. Though they often appear resistant to change, they are frequently transformed. Objectives, activities, and organizational structures change, and organizations sometimes drift into forms remarkably different from the original."

March suggests that organizational change arises primarily in reaction to external factors. Just as an individual's workday is often shaped by interruptions and crises, the character of an institution is vulnerable to pressures from without. Policies, priorities, and resources thus become a function of the circumstance that captures momentary attention.

Second Assumption: Change in Postsecondary Education Comes Gradually. Evidence of this assumption is abundant throughout community college education. Our colleges often appear bewildered at the burgeoning needs of society. Marked by bureaucratic lethargy, institutions frequently struggle to apply resources to demands that have long since passed. Seldom are these external developments rationalized or predicted by the college hierarchy, and the corresponding sense of insecurity has a profound effect on clientele. Sikes and others (1974, p. 19) describe this phenomenon succinctly: "Human problems generated by institutional uncertainty are numerous. On many campuses, the inhabitants feel lonely, isolated, hostile, competitive, insecure, and anxious. They often feel powerless to change 'the establishment' in order to control their own lives. Institutions, by and large, offer few opportunities for individuals to shape themselves and their environments. Campuses offer little encouragement for simultaneously learning to comprehend, to feel and to create, to take risks and to behave autonomously."

At present, postsecondary educational environments often serve to inhibit the change process. Yet, the need for community college education to become more quickly and responsively in step with outside forces is clearly intensifying. Nothing less than institutional survival may be at stake.

Third Assumption: Change in Society Comes Rapidly — and Must be Managed. Since Toffler (1981) brought futurism into the public consciousness, Americans have been coming to grips with the realization that tomorrow is indeed today. Most of today's community college leaders were in graduate school during the 1960s, at the onset of the information revolution that ushered in Toffler's "Third Wave." As it gathered momentum, many in the vanguard joined the postsecondary labor force, taking positions that would ultimately lead to prominence. Unfortunately, this left today's leaders chained to their desks, even as the technolgical upheaval produced computerized data retrieval, worldwide telecommunication, and instant change. Community college administrators were faced with the challenge of simultaneously keeping up with and staying ahead of the massive information crescendo. Due to their visible positions, they were also charged with responsibility for aligning leadership with the chemistry of change and with organizational structure and mission in order to advance their institutions while at the same time producing future leaders.

The nature of this dynamic amalgam of responsibilities has never been completely identified. Rather, the treadmill of daily office life simply does not give leaders time to create a nourishing organizational climate in which future leadership is able to develop. This fact has much to do with the relation between stability and creativity. While necessity may be the mother of invention, few innovations or inventions are the products of an unstable environment. In the environment that prevails today, faculty and staff will not be driven to arrive at uncommon solutions to common problems. It thus falls to community college leaders to fashion an atmosphere that can both accommodate change and ensure personal security.

Fourth Assumption: Some Leadership Skills Are Trainable. According to March (1980), certain leadership competencies can be reduced to teachable units. First, there are roughly two types of knowledge: that which we possess and that which we know where to find. The effective leader has a realistic grasp of both, having accumulated the former and identified the latter. It would be ludicrous for a college president to make an intelligent decision about a computer while relying on a minimal understanding of the system's capabilities and the human factors involved. Leaders must eventually obtain testimony to move beyond two or more staff members or external consultants who claim that a solution requires their services. Second, a leader must often seek information that is extremely sensitive and not easy to cull. Nonetheless, through skillful inquiry, a dean or vice-president can avoid the political heat that comes from advancing an undeveloped and naive proposition. Questioning techniques can be mastered through study and practice. Third, leaders recognize that conflict must occur in any organization. Rather than to deny its inevitability, the astute manager develops competence in the areas of negotiation, communication, and conflict resolution. Perhaps the pursuit of understanding between individuals or groups is a luxury, but it never stops being worthwhile. Fourth, long before the word *politics* became synonymous with shrewdness and chicanery, it conveyed the image of human interaction in quest of the common good. Thus, the information of coalitions is merely a visible result of human nature. Skill in working effectively with both small and large groups is of paramount importance to any administrator. Once again, certain competencies in this area can be taught, including problem clarification, options, development and analysis, and role differentiation. These features, combined with intuition, courage, and eloquence, should produce a brand of leadership that replaces vision with pluralistic understanding. Fifth, issue management is another important leadership skill. The political process has always been issue-oriented. Taking full advantage of that process requires the identification and effective management of issues with the press, legislature, governor's office, and so forth, to orchestrate a positive resolution. Community college leaders must begin to think in terms of broad issues and teach faculty and staff to do likewise.

Fifth Assumption: Change Comes from the Desire for Improvement. While it is possible to learn certain leadership skills, positive change cannot come without motivation. The greatest obstacle to change is not scarce resources but the unwillingness of organizational members to make the attempt. An insecure environment can inhibit creativity and initiative, since participants often believe that unpredictable restrictions will somehow appear. This feeling may originate from politicization within the institution that is beyond the control of its members. Institutional leaders must massage these situations, so that educational issues emerge from and are separated from political issues.

Unlocking the mystery of human motivation is a constant challenge to any leader. The classic springboard to organizational creativity is the development of an environment that promotes trust and guarantees equitable treatment. Faculty and staff must feel that they are valued as the organization's greatest resource. To bring this about, leaders must employ the right mixture of confidence and patience in order to delegate responsibilities and sensitively see them through.

Within this trusting relationship, however, the inevitability of change must be clearly understood. While staff members should feel professionally comfortable, they must also realize that their present skills may not always be valued as the institution grows. The impact of this realization can be positive or negative. A community college that carefully and consciously provides alternative career paths, flexible benefits, retraining opportunities, and early retirement programs has gone a long way in promoting a stable but dynamic environment.

Finally, much has been written about the inability of this nation to instill a sense of organizational loyalty in its labor force. This inability is a basic indictment of our leadership, a statement on its short-sightedness and often dysfunctional administrative practices. While participatory management (as embodied, for example, in quality circles) may not succeed in every situation, its insistence on shared responsibility should serve to increase pride, productivity, and loyalty. Unquestionably, loyalty is the one thing that a leader cannot do without.

Sixth Assumption: Important Change Is Externally Driven. The traditional American notion of leadership, which March (1980) disputes, is that excellence at the top initiates extraordinary internal change. While this belief is gratifying to the ego, current reality indicates that the exact opposite is true. Much of our present community college leadership, whether good or bad, arises almost by accident and is primarily reactive in nature. Chancellors and presidents rarely originate great institutional accomplishments. For every William Rainey Harper and Daniel Coit Gilman there are dozens of understated competent administrators trying to preserve order against chaos. Few of their organizational strategies or leadership initiatives will make much difference to the destiny of their institution. Rather, their contribution may often be shaped in response to an external issue: the abrupt shift of financial aid policy in Washington, a serious economic recession, or the shutdown of a nearby business installation.

Neither do chief executive officers react solely to off-campus stimuli. Within the institution, they are constantly presented with staff propositions for consideration, some undoubtedly of high quality. Few would disagree with the proposition that the better the staff, the better the leadership appears. Moreover, many colleges frequently house "hidden" leaders — competent people who are never formally identified or who choose not to be. Thus, as March (1980, p. 2) states, "organizations rarely do exactly what they are told to do." Since many of the mishandled directives emanate from the leadership, presidents and chancellors who view themselves as the source of change are in for a frustrating experience. Thus, it seems more likely that effective leadership lies in the ability to keep one's ear to the ground—although not for so long that one fails to provide visible leadership for faculty and staff.

Strategies for Leadership Development

The problem of leadership for community colleges has two dimensions. The leadership traits required for the next century have as yet received little attention. Indeed, no systematic leadership development process has been set in motion since the Kellogg Foundation program in the 1960s.

National Responses. In order to address leadership development for community colleges, a national commission should be formed to examine the future leadership requirements of the American community college movement. This body might study the career patterns and impact of former Kellogg fellows. It could review the current organizational climate in community college education and discuss future directions. It could analyze the effects of the information revolution on postsecondary education needs. It could examine national and international demographic, political, and economic trends, and it could conduct extensive research on community college districts in a variety of settings, including both urban and rural.

Assuming that two decades is a reasonable gestation period for training leadership to attain positions of prominence and develop what March (1980) calls "uncommon imagination," it is imperative that formal training centers be established very soon. They must be interdisciplinary in outlook. Future leaders must internalize diverse types of knowledge: the sociology of organizations, political processes accompanying change, management of coalitions, proper translation of external forces, and, most important, methods that allow internal creativity to flourish. They must fully realize that change is inevitable. If leaders are to manage change processes in the tumultuous period ahead, this diverse knowledge must be operationalized.

Local Responses. Unfortunately, community colleges cannot wait for the establishment of a national commission and leadership training centers. Districts and individual colleges must begin their own efforts to facilitate adjustment to an uncertain future, to improve institutional quality in an uncertain present, and to develop leaders. At a minimum, two steps are required: staff renewal and management flexibilities. The need for staff renewal is obvious in this period of job burnout, productivity lags, and adversarial relationships between labor and management. Community colleges exist to provide for the growth and renewal of a student population. Potential leaders must be afforded similar opportunities if they are to service the clientele effectively. Community colleges must provide staff renewal opportunities that can assist developing leaders to come to a clear understanding of their capabilities, strengths, and weaknesses. As a result of such activity, leaders will become aware of behavior patterns that are inappropriate for the solution of emerging problems.

In a business that extols the virtues of individual potential, a consistent management policy would provide various performance options. New forms of recognition for emerging leaders should be explored, as should policies covering liberalized leave for advanced education and professional development. Community colleges might want to experiment with such techniques as flextime and job sharing to free emerging leaders for professional development.

Conclusion

A crisis is developing at the leadership level of the American community college movement. We need a crystallized definition of the characteristics and skills that the next crop of leaders must possess. However, there is currently no organized mechanism for leadership training, such as existed at the Kellogg Foundation in the 1960s. In this chapter, I have outlined five assumptions about leadership in order to sketch a framework for future consideration and action.

The question of leadership inevitably returns to the manner in which organizational change is managed. Like individuals, organizations evolve at varying rates. Postsecondary institutions have traditionally lagged behind other sectors of society, such as technology and industry. The creation of centers for the study of community college leadership is of practical and paramount importance, since many of the skills that future leaders will need can be developed by training. If innovation at the community college level is to continue, those who will break new ground must excel in the areas of politics, conflict resolution, motivation, and response to external change.

The future contains both hopes and dangers. Whether we collide with change or manage to pull order out of chaos remains to be seen. But, we can build a coherent approach to the future by studying present trends. Once these trends have been grasped, leadership must begin to fashion proactive, change-oriented responses. The first phase of this effort has been the major theme of this chapter: discussion about the character of individuals who will be the custodians of our nation's educational ideals and establishment of community college leadership centers. On the local level, the first steps involve increased attention to staff renewal and flexible management designs.

Through coordinated and well-planned efforts, effective leadership can chart a path to future institutional health. Those currently at the top cannot relax for a moment. Leadership, we may be reminded, is action, not position. Meaningful action requires courage and persistence. The talent questionably exists. It is time to return our attention to leadership.

References

March, J. *Footnotes to Organizational Change.* Project Report No. 80-A6. Stanford, Calif.: Public Institute for Research on Educational Finance and Governance, School of Education, Stanford University, 1980.

Sikes, W. W., Schlesinger, L. E., and Seashore, E. N. *Renewing Higher Education from Within: A Guide for Campus Change Teams.* San Francisco: Jossey-Bass, 1974.

Toffler, A. *The Third Wave.* New York: Bantam, 1981.

Paul A. Elsner is chancellor of the Maricopa County (Arizona) Community College District.

PART 2.

Providing Effective Leadership in an Era of Transition

The role of the community college leader today is complex and multifaceted. It involves the use of communications technology, considerable dependence on data for decision making, and working with a myriad of external organizations.

Dimensions of Change Confronting Institutional Leaders

Robert H. McCabe

For the past three decades, America has been in a period of dramatic change. Perhaps the single most important characteristic that we live with today is the constancy of change: Our world is in continual transition, and there is little prospect of stabilizing in the near future. Major events of the past and the rapidity of social evolution are reflected in an amazingly resilient and adaptive nation.

Following World War II, there was a period of great economic expansion and national euphoria. In the decades that followed, the nation has struggled to overcome its past treatment of minorities. The stalling of economic development paralleled the era of the Vietnam War, Watergate, and Nixon. That stalling was followed by high inflation, which was caused by many factors, including the OPEC-driven oil shortage and substantial increases in the cost of energy. Third World countries are reaching for larger shares of the world's goods and economy, and the reconstructed industries of Japan and other countries are providing fierce international competition.

The demographics of our country have changed dramatically. The birth rate has dropped, especially among whites, and the numbers of minorities are increasing. The movement of population into the

R. L. Alfred, P. A. Elsner, R. J. LeCroy, N. Armes (Eds.). *Emerging Roles for Community College Leaders.*
New Directions for Community Colleges, no. 46. San Francisco: Jossey-Bass, June 1984.

large urban areas has stabilized and in some cases reversed. Behind all these significant social changes are inescapable facts of our present life — an overpowering realization of the constant threat of nuclear holocaust and the rather recent recognition that, since as early as 1970, we have been in an unsettling transformation from an industrial to an information age economy.

The accelerated evolution in our society over the past three decades parallels the most significant era of growth and development for the American community college. During the brief history of the community college movement, public attitudes toward social programs have seen some dramatic shifts. Today, the feeling that social programs have not worked, that there is too much government regulation, and that people should do more for themselves is strong. Yet, the problems of urban areas and minority populations have not lessened. Rather, the changing requirements for literacy in an information age and the stress of the substantial transitions that society is undergoing have caused already severe problems to deepen. Any public institution, especially one as closely tied to the needs of society as the community college, will also find itself deeply immersed in transition. Thus, the role of community college leaders in the mid 1980s must be significantly different, both in scope and content, from what it was in the expansion years of the 1950s and 1960s.

Community Colleges and Adaptation

The community colleges are just beginning to reach maturity, along with the individuals who began their careers in these institutions. The work on facilities and campuses has been completed, and faculty and staff are well trained and experienced. The natural reaction would be to hold on tightly to concepts and programs that worked effectively in the past. Yet, it is essential to preserve a second important principle, adaptation. The great expansion of the community college movement did not result from a static program but from a program that responded quickly to the needs of a changing society. Undefined in mission, without traditions, and with strong funding, community colleges performed whatever functions seemed to be necessary. Because of the excellent match of jobs and programs in an expanding and increasingly complex economy, our institutions received accolades for their efforts. However, as America progresses through the information age and as world and society and economies undergo some fundamental changes, community colleges must continue to adapt and provide programs that communities need and support.

Unfortunately, many leaders appear to be mentally stuck in the attitudes of the 1960s, when colleges worked to achieve access, some-times at the expense of completion and attainment. Many practices followed in the 1960s became increasingly inappropriate in the 1970s. High school graduates and new clientele reflecting a lack of emphasis or attainment in elementary and secondary education enrolled in large numbers. These new students had fewer academic skills, while in-dustry was demanding more. Like other urban community colleges, Miami-Dade Community College evolved into an institution that not only provided open access but an open-flow educational model as well. There were fewer requirements, most students were self-advised, and practices were based on the idea that students knew best what was right for them and that counseling should be nondirective. Faculty and administrators talked about the right to fail—tacit agreement that staff were not well equipped to predict what students could achieve—and upheld students' rights to choose classes, set their own directions, and make changes as they desired.

In the 1970s, several additional factors emerged that were important in community college development. One of these factors was the continued increase in federally based financial aid. In the low- or no-fee community colleges, students with Basic Educational Oppor-tunity Grants actually received cash for living allowances. As clientele continued to change, students became less prepared academically, and increasingly representative of new groups—minorities, women, handi-capped, and older citizens. Added to the generalized mistrust of authority and institutions that grew out of the Nixon–Vietnam War era, these factors changed the climate and circumstances that predomi-nated during the growth years of America's community colleges.

Other important changes are now taking place. As America enters the information age, the number of unskilled and semiskilled jobs is declining, and a growing number of jobs are requiring informa-tion skills—defining, reading, analyzing, interpreting, applying, and communicating information. Communities are faced with a dilemma: Jobs require more information skills, and Americans possess fewer of these skills. Individuals who want to advance their education but have the least preparation to do so are enrolled principally in community colleges. Community colleges may fail to meet the resulting challenge—that of successfully providing quality education in open-access institu-tions that equips competent graduates with the skills needed to meet the demands of information age industry and business. The open-flow model of the open-access institution has little prospect of working in this environment. Drastic changes in the operational structure and ap-proach are essential if community colleges are to contribute to the economic and social development of the nation by salvaging opportunity for large numbers of citizens whose skills are inappropriate or inadequate for the times.

Elements of a New Institutional Environment

The Federal Government. To a great extent, the federal government has provided the impetus for expansion in community colleges through programs that help students to attend and that regulate access and opportunity. However, changes initiated under the Reagan administration could alter the past pattern of growth. Changing public attitudes place increased emphasis on merit and individual responsibility and express suspicion of the benefits of social programs.

The Reagan administration expanded financial aid in the area of guaranteed student loans. This expansion principally benefits middle- and higher-income students at independent four-year colleges and universities. At the same time, it introduced a number of restrictive practices—limits on the Pell grant program and establishment of time-based standards of progress so that students are expected to complete programs within a given amount of time. These developments are counter to the idea that students who begin with deficiencies require more time to complete a program. They are, however, consistent with a growing public feeling that money should not be wasted on the unprepared. Further, the federal government has revised its regulatory and auditing procedures to place greater pressure on institutions to tighten their administration of financial aid programs. The concept of applying regulations of general application to institutions that receive federal funds is a clear expansion of rule making, which is most evident in issues dealing with access and opportunity.

The States. While the federal government fueled the access revolution, state governments provided most of the funds to institutions for operations. In many states, community colleges have been funded from a combination of local and state tax bases. Surprisingly, most colleges have been able to operate with considerable local autonomy, despite the high level of state support. This pattern is now changing. As state revenues fail to keep pace with the myriad of needs that citizens expect to be financed with government funds, there is greater scrutiny of the expenditure of these funds, and competition among priorities increases. Legislators will seek—and obtain—more control over the programs that they are funding.

States are increasingly concerned about duplication of effort, and consequently they are increasing their efforts to coordinate institutions from a centralized point. The cost of these coordinating efforts, especially if they are line operations rather than institutional cooperatives, always exceeds any possible savings. The cost of coordination affects all levels. Responsiveness slows, data-collection and reporting requirements increase, new staff are required at the central level and matching staff are required at the institutional level, and staff at lower levels in the organization increasingly feel impotent. The systematization of community colleges seems clearly evident in the development of new state boards with increased authority. California and Florida are good examples. In a recent article for the Orange County (California) *Daily Pilot,* Bernard Luskin (1984), president of Orange Coast Community College, identified a growing problem: "Now community colleges are 'state-funded institutions,' and with state funds has come a continuing blizzard of regulation and more centralization of power, exposing even stronger trends toward state control."

A factor that further complicates the educational decision-making process and that places it at higher levels is the broadly held feeling among politicians, citizens, and interest groups that educational institutions have not done a good job. This continually reinforced public opinion has made legislatures, state boards, and state bureaucracies increasingly willing to make decisions about community college policy. The impact of this trend extends to curriculum and instructional methods, which have always been the prerogative of the institution and faculty. Members of state bureaucracies often lack experience in the educational system and a full understanding of institutional mission and goals. Their objectives are often negative—to determine areas in which funding can be reduced, to search for identifiable misuse of funds, or to uncover an improper computation in an allocation formula.

Given the current public concern with the effectiveness of open-access policies and with the breadth of program offerings, the community college mission faces some serious issues. In most cases, the mission of community colleges is better understood and appreciated in local communities than at the state level, where community colleges must compete with the universities. It is difficult to make a case for the prestige of institutions that are open to all, despite the great contribution made to society when individuals who begin with deficiencies become productive citizens. It is much easier to appreciate the contribution of the community college and to be supportive at the local level, where graduates are employed, where students attend classes, and where student's friends, neighbors, and relatives often have benefited from attendance at the same college. Thus, maximum local control and participation in funding is a significant benefit to community colleges.

The Local Board and Community. As community colleges have become integrated into large systems, boards have had to assume very different roles. Today, there is more direct involvement, more difficulty in carrying out the complex monitoring role, and more tension between boards and administration, staff, and faculty than there was in the earlier days. While change is evident in both appointed and elected boards, elected board members are often under special pressure to consider the role of staff and faculty in the election process. Since the election of community college board often fails to capture broad public interest, employee groups, especially faculty, are becoming an important base of support for board candidates.

Members of boards are not immune from the public concern for quality. Thus, they are interested in receiving more data and information as well as in greater participation in program decisions. As the state legislature has increased its control over institutional operations, a new political dimension has been added to the administration of community colleges. The board is now required to deal with the legislature, state boards, and state bureaucracies. Strong efforts in image building have become essential in order to develop a positive public attitude toward the institution that can be translated into legislative support.

Internal or Institutional Concerns. The restrictions on decision-making authority and the increased controls that community college leaders face today are extraordinary. The situation in Florida well illustrates them. The state legislature is deeply involved in institutional decision making, ranging from the definition of mission to the design of specific courses. Today, a bureaucracy in the state department of education has specific administrative responsibilities, collects data, and represents the state commissioner of education and the state department of education to the institutions. This represents a significant change from years past, when the same organization represented the institutions and their goals and objectives to the legislature and the commissioner.

There is also an appointed state board of community colleges, a local district board of trustees, a comprehensive vocational coordinating council for the region that includes both public schools and community colleges, and a state board of education comprised of the members of the state cabinet. In addition, there are advisory committees for each occupational program, an alumni association, a foundation board, faculty senates (in some institutions a faculty union), and staff employee councils. The individual college is further regulated by the federal government through funded programs, by directives from the Equal Employment Commission, and by the state's public employee relations commission. The resulting network is even more complex for Miami-Dade Community College, since its system encompasses a district administration, campus administrations, faculty senates on each campus, and a senate consortium for the whole institution. There are also student governments. Presidents must also deal with city and county governments and organized special-interest groups in the ongoing operation of their institutions.

One of the most difficult areas in the new environment with which they must deal is the area of faculty concerns. Hiring has slowed considerably as growth has slowed, and institutions have been using more part-time faculty in order to maintain flexibility or save money. There has also been a significant change in clientele. New students have different needs, motivations, and educational goals. Programs are shifting too, as the declining enrollment in such subjects as history and foreign language shows.

Finance is another problem that affects faculty morale. During the 1960s, salaries increased at a rate exceeding inflation. During the 1970s, however, support for higher education declined, and salaries failed to keep pace with inflation. Between the 1976–77 and the 1982–83 academic years, the gap between the rise in the Consumer Price Index and increases in faculty salaries increased by nearly five times ("Faculty Pay and the Cost of Living," 1984). During the same period, salaries of other nonagricultural employees kept pace with the index. As this pattern continues over the years, concern has grown. Failure to meet inflation by 1 percent, 2 percent, or 3 percent every year produces a major discrepancy between income and costs, which becomes a constant source of stress and worry. In urban areas, this pattern has forced many faculty into part-time employment outside the college and consequently reduced their commitment to the institution and to students.

New Operational Approaches

Of the many considerations affecting the way in which community college leaders must operate today, the most important is the ability to maintain a broad perspective on issues. The institution, its mission, its image, its priorities, its relationship to society, and its place in the larger educational system are all critical concerns. More than at any other time, the leader must be an educational visionary and keep the focus directed on the essential purposes and value of the institution. As the institution's goals and mission are challenged, the leader must continually emphasize the important contributions of the open-door community college. However, he or she must also be realistic in analyzing the prospect for success in matching the institution's educational program with the requirements of society. In this period of rapid change, individuals and groups are becoming increasingly assertive about the roles that they see for community colleges. To permit external groups to shape the destiny of the institutions would surely result in weakness and failure. It is the responsibility of the leader to set the course for the future.

Working with Constituents. A significant amount of the leader's time must be devoted to establishing rapport and working with various constituents in the community—business and industry groups, community leaders, political figures, governmental agencies, and so forth. Local legislators must be helped to become fully cognizant of the institution's mission and benefits, its goals, and the importance of its services to the community. To accomplish this task, assistance from a broad range of local leaders is needed. Legislators reflect public attitudes. It is important for there to be a positive attitude in the community toward the institution and for local leaders to be willing to stand up as advocates. While the development of support is a public relations function, it must be based on performance and on a good match between programs and community needs and aspirations.

Fund raising is one important way of building local support. It provides a platform, a reason to talk to leaders, and a reason to explain the institution and what it does. Of course, there are times when a platform can be attained by other methods. A good example is the millage referendum recently held in Cleveland for the Cuyahoga Community College District, which provided a reason to talk specifically about the institution with groups throughout the community for a period of more than a year.

Today, a community college leader must be prepared to deal with the media. He or she must understand that individuals in the media often are interested in negative stories, because such stories sell newspapers. Therefore, it is necessary to build a cordial and positive relationship with members of the media and to be available and willing to discuss issues. More important, if negative information arises, the institution needs to release the appropriate information rather than allowing it to leak out in some less credible way. Thus, it is a good idea to visit the editorial boards of major newspapers once every six months to discuss the college and its goals as well as issues that the public should be informed about. While these visits do not always result in helpful articles or editorials, they help to develop working relationships with individuals who are very important to the cultivation of an institutional image.

Information. One of the greatest changes affecting community college administration today involves the availability and abundance of information. The new and ever expanding communications technology makes it easy to access vast amounts of information. Requirements for reporting and analysis have increased, and external agencies rely heavily on the data that they collect in order to make decisions, regardless of the quality of these data. Thus, it becomes extremely important to exercise care in the research process, so that data will be accurate, they will be collected in accord with uniform standards, and they will reflect what is happening in the institution. Data can be misused, and they frequently are. For example, in Florida, data in a state report classified student assistants as administrative support personnel. If a legislative aide had interpreted these data at face value, the legislature would have received a completely distorted picture of the relationship between the number of administrative support personnel and faculty.

A final major concern about the increased availability of information is that information is expensive to collect and maintain. The development of information systems is an arduous, time-consuming, and costly task, but it is necessary to ensure accurate data input and proper maintenance. Further, organized data provide the institution with important opportunities to know more about its operations and thus to make better decisions. Unfortunately, administrators are often so bogged down in collecting and reporting information that they make little constructive use of the data in their own decisions.

Application of Systems Technology to Education. Our educational system is really a combination of human interaction and information exchange. The application of systems technology to instruction and academic support services is essential if community colleges are to bring large numbers of unprepared students to higher levels of performance. To illustrate, the order in which courses should be taken and students should move through the system is designed at the institutional level at Miami-Dade. Students are tested at admission, and if they are deficient in basic skills, they are assigned to necessary developmental course work. Student performance is consistently monitored under standards of academic progress. As early as seven credits, load restrictions are added, and supportive services and directive counseling are provided. On completion of seventeen credits, additional restrictions are imposed in order to match students with an appropriate course load so that they can proceed successfully through the system. If they are still not progressing satisfactorily at thirty credits, suspensions are used.

Through a computerized academic alert system, all students receive an individualized letter approximately six weeks into each term. These letters are based on information from faculty about students' current status and academic progress. The comprehensive application of communications technology makes it possible to advise students on an ongoing basis. Advisement is stratified, with counselors assisting students who have the most difficult problems. Advisers who deal only with academic advisement see all new students as well as those who fall under any of the standards of academic progress restrictions just outlined. Faculty members advise the remaining students. Students receive a computer-generated Advisement/Graduation Information System (AGIS) printout, on which the transcript is ordered by requirement rather than by term. The AGIS report provides data on students' standing in relation to each requirement, as well as other individualized information. Using a grid based on the major, the AGIS printout also shows the other courses required for the major at the institution to which the individual intends to transfer. Thus, students can know at any given time how far they have moved toward graduation requirements. Additional prescriptions in course order and course volume are currently being added to the AGIS system to increase the ability of faculty members to advise properly and accurately.

All these monitoring and support programs depend on the use of communications technology to make them economically practical. The entire system is controlled by the use of computerized information in the process of registration and enrollment. Management systems currently in operation include productivity analysis and assignment, continued monitoring toward registration goals, forecasting of long-term needs, and budgets and cash management. All these components form part of any business enterprise in the 1980s.

Conclusion

The role of the community college leader is complex and multi-faceted. It involves the knowledgeable use of communications technology, considerable dependence on data for decision making, and working with a myriad of external organizations. For the leader, one of the greatest dangers is that of allowing the demands of written and oral correspondence to control his or her time and work. It is important not to be trapped by the expectations and requirements of others, because this allows them to establish the priorities. The leader must avoid this ever present threat, carefully delegate tasks, and rely on other members of the staff to maintain the routine flow of work. Quality individuals need and deserve the discretion to make decisions and to participate in creative activity. Only by delegating authority can the leader acquire the time that he or she must devote to work with national and state legislatures, local community groups and representatives, the board of trustees, and individuals within the institution. The leader must be in a position to set his or her own priorities.

Most important, the leader must never relinquish the role of educational visionary. He or she must fully undertand the place of the institution in the fabric of American society and understand the changing dynamics of society and community so that the right decisions about the role and direction of the institution can be made. The institution must have a spokesperson. The leader is the only individual within the institution who is in a position to envision the larger issues concerning educational practice and policy. All other individuals in the institution will view the issues from more specific and thus narrower perspectives. While these perspectives are important, and they should be given consideration, the leader must maintain the comprehensive understanding and personal vision required to guide the educational program. This is especially vital in the present period of constant change both in the larger society and in our own institutions.

References

"Faculty Pay and the Cost of Living." *Chronicle of Higher Education.* January 4, 1984, p. 21.
Luskin, B. "Outlook 1984." Orange County (California) *Daily Pilot,* January 23, 1984, unnumbered supplement.

Robert H. McCabe is president of Miami-Dade Community College in Miami, Florida.

As the student population changes, community colleges
experience substantial changes in both policy and operations.
Whether these changes are instituted from within or without
is a critical task for leadership.

Leadership and Community Change

Joshua L. Smith

Communities are in a state of continuous change. Community colleges are directly affected by changes in the communities where they are located. By virtue of their mission, community colleges should change as their clientele and community change. These issues do not need to be debated. However, it is difficult for community college leaders to answer some other questions: Which societal changes are significant and why? Which community changes are significant and why? Do these changes have relevance to the mission of the institution? What responses would be appropriate for the institution? What new or additional resources would be needed in order to respond? How are we to evaluate the changes put into place? What new needs or demands will these changes create?

Community college leaders find it difficult to answer these questions, which on the surface seem perfectly reasonable, because the answers represent some admixture of fact and fiction, perception and reality, and philosophy and pragmatism. That is, answers to these questions constitute administrative efforts to impose order on variety, and they are as much a function of leader perception of their causes as they are a reflection of individual and collective ability to manipulate the environment.

R. L. Alfred, P. A. Elsner, R. J. LeCroy, N. Armes (Eds.). *Emerging Roles for Community College Leaders.*
New Directions for Community Colleges, no. 46. San Francisco: Jossey-Bass, June 1984.

This chapter uses examples drawn from an urban community college to illustrate changes in the demography, social structure, and educational needs of the communities served by community colleges. Community change is examined from three perspectives: the changing educational needs of specific community constituencies as new social, economic, and technological trends emerge, institutional responses to these changing needs, and the implications of these responses for leadership.

Changing Community Needs

The new student now occupying a majority of the chairs in community colleges is a product of changes taking place in communities across the country. It is almost axiomatic in our society that as the federal government reduces or eliminates its spending on human services, unemployment and enrollment in postsecondary education and training programs increase. History verifies this corollary relationship repeatedly. Examined in the context of the urban community, it is a fact of life that during the past two decades there has been a steady out-migration of middle- and upper-middle-income families and a steady inmigration of impoverished, needy families into inner cities. As the numbers of poor, alienated, foreign-born, unemployed, and single-parent families increase in our urban centers, crime also increases. In successive, ongoing waves, ethnic enclaves become ethnic strongholds as immigrants and others seek solace and fortification within bonded groups based on race, origin, color, religious belief, and other anti-melting pot factors. Ghettoes based on language, race, ethnicity, origin, poverty, and other factors now abound in most metropolitan areas throughout the United States.

Student Population Characteristics. With the advent of change in the population base of communities has come a significant change in the characteristics of students served by community colleges, particularly by those located in urban regions. Between 1970 and 1978, enrollment of black students increased by 30 percent, while that of Hispanics increased by 65 percent. At present, it is estimated that blacks constitute 10 percent and that Hispanics constitute 6 percent of the total community college population. In addition to the black and Hispanic students, the minority representation in community colleges is increasing as numbers of "new immigrants" from Mexico, Central America, Latin America, the Caribbean, and the Orient are added. Along with their cultural differences, the new immigrants, as well as other students for whom English is not the primary language, bring sharply increased demands for instruction in English as a second language.

In the past ten years, the number of minority students in elementary and secondary education has seen a startling increase. A recent Council of Great City Schools report places the increase in minority students in Dade County, Florida, at 43 percent, in Minneapolis at 50 percent, and in Long Beach, California at 129 percent. Asian student enrollment has increased by 256 percent nationally, representing 745,000 students in elementary and secondary schools in 1980. The result is that minorities now constitute 57 percent of the elementary and secondary enrollment in New Mexico and 43 percent of the elementary and secondary enrollment in California. When we consider the displaced workers, single parents, returning adult learners, first-generation college attendees, and displaced homemakers whose needs must also be considered when we design postsecondary programs and services, we appreciate that community college leaders face difficult problems with respect to the mix of programs and services, academic standards and policies, and cost-benefit equations that can be applied to a diverse student body.

Literacy. The nontraditional students who are an increasing percentage of all community college students are notably underprepared for college-level work. A steadily increasing percentage requires developmental and remedial services before college-level work can be undertaken successfully. Although community college students may have great developmental needs, it is important to note that they differ from other college-bound students primarily in severity of need. Public schools, especially in the urban centers, have not succeeded in graduating students prepared adequately either for direct employment or for some form of postsecondary education. High school graduation grade point averages, coupled with national College Entrance Examination Board scores, indicate not only that graduating seniors are achieving less well in high school but also that fewer students envision college or some form of postsecondary education after high school and that steadily increasing numbers of high school graduates have no plans for the future at all. There is further evidence of this trend in the results of examinations administered to persons interested in military service, data from which indicate that an alarming preponderance of applicants cannot read above sixth-grade level or add a single column of numbers correctly, with or without the benefit of a high school diploma or the GED certificate. Rejected for military service, ineligible for welfare and other social service benefits, unemployed and unemployable, but still believing in the dream of education as the ultimate equalizer in our society, these persons are enrolling in community colleges throughout the United States in steadily increasing numbers.

Technology. The 1980s ushered in an era in which technology will be applied to industrial tasks — a development that will result in the dislocation and relocation of thousands of workers as the labor force is restructured to meet emerging needs. Naisbitt (1982) analyzes changes in the labor force: "The real increase in positions has been in the information occupations. In 1950, only about 17 percent of the work force was engaged in information jobs. Now, more than 60 percent work with information as programmers, teachers, clerks, secretaries, accountants, stock brokers, managers, insurance agents, bureaucrats, lawyers, bankers, and technicians. . . most Americans spend their time creating, processing, or distributing information."

In both industry and agriculture, automation is increasing unemployment, as planters, pickers, and packers are replaced by automated machinery, as typesetters are displaced by computerized composer-printers, and as robots weld and test automobiles on the production line. And, the microprocessor is far more threatening to the stability of the old order than even the early applications of computer technology. Futurists in Britain claim that the microprocessor already has infiltrated 38 percent of the world's present economy. Naisbitt (1982, p. 29) states that *Newsweek* magazine recently estimated that between 50 and 75 percent of all U.S. factory workers could be displaced by robots before the end of the century. Others watching the telecommunications industry project similar progress worldwide and rapid displacement of people and jobs by the microprocessor in particular and by computer technology in general.

Technology is not static. It is continually evolving, expanding, miniaturizing, and altering the world that we know. The technical jobs for which community colleges are training students are in many instances technologically obsolete. Thus, community colleges must continually assess and reassess needs and trends in the workplaces where they expect to place graduates, and at the same time they must assess their own students' needs. Student assessment is extremely important, as the skill profiles of entering students show. With Scholastic Aptitude Test scores at an all-time low, and as the number of entering students who cannot read, speak, or write acceptable English or pass a simple arithmetic competence examination increases, the goal of preparing students for high-technology jobs in an information-processing society becomes distant and costly. Without basic skills, computer literacy is out of the question. Moreover, since technology is changing the world of work at a staggering rate, it is imperative for community colleges to provide their graduates with a conceptual knowledge on which they can build and with a desire to be reeducated throughout their work lives.

Lifelong Learning. One of the most dramatic and visible changes now under way in postsecondary education is the growing orientation to lifelong learning of every ilk and variety, ranging from Erhard Seminars Training and religious cults to the Scarsdale Diet, language learning tapes for automobile drivers, and a staggering array of school-based courses offered by continuing education offices on campuses across the country. Whether from a love for learning, a desire to acquire new skills, a need to fill lonely hours, an attempt to get a promotion or a new and better job, or some combination of all these, people are returning to community colleges, universities, proprietary schools, YMCAs and YWCAs, churches, travel and tour groups, and other sources for continuous learning. Without a doubt, lifelong learning and continuing self-improvement will continue to swell the ranks and increase the variety of students who enroll in formal and informal programs of learning at community colleges.

Requisites for Management

Community colleges by definition serve the community. Consequently, as the changes described in the preceding section change the student population, the colleges themselves experience substantial changes in both policy and operations. Whether these changes are instituted from within or without the community college is a critical task for management.

The most far-reaching change that a majority of community colleges have instituted is the implementation of the open-admissions policy to accommodate rapidly changing community needs. The open-admissions policy has profound effects on the management, structure, staffing, governance, operations, and funding of community colleges. First and foremost, it places an overwhelming demand on community colleges for remedial services, which affects their productivity and effectiveness. When lack of proficiency in the English language is coupled with severe need for basic skills training, student progress is expectedly slow—especially in view of the debate still under way about the most effective methods of teaching English as a second language and in view of resource limitations that prohibit one-on-one instruction in skills courses. Like traditional students, nontraditional community college students often resist taking skills courses, preferring the high-status credit courses that define the taker as matriculating toward a degree. Thus, as a direct corollary of the open-admissions policy and its consequences, a majority of community colleges have found it essential to reevaluate, rethink, and restructure their support services.

For remediation, the major issues are how to develop, strengthen, and reinforce the basic skills required for success in college-level work across the curriculum in a manner that is both effective and cost-efficient. In addition to rethinking traditional remedial classroom instructional modes, materials, and teaching techniques, explorations include application of computer technology and tutorial programs (both human and machine-based) to learning laboratories and other self-paced learning modalities that will enable students to remedy their skill deficiencies as quickly and effectively as possible.

For testing and evaluation, the major issues are the development and standardization of non-culturally biased evaluation and testing instruments and procedures that accurately and fairly assess skill deficiencies independent of language or test-taking proficiency. The development of diagnostic and prescriptive test instruments linked directly to curricular sequences that can enhance placement and students' progress is extremely important.

For counseling, the major issues are predicting, understanding, retraining, and redeploying college resources — counseling faculty — so that the real needs of the new students can be met. Since it now is frequently the case that community colleges are attracting increasing numbers of students who are the first in their family to attend college and a majority of these first-time college students lack information about college routines and requirements and about career and degree requirements, there is a critical need to reconceptualize and redeploy counseling resources so that they are available to all entering students at the moment of entry into the community college environment and continuously thereafter. Orientation programs, personal and career counseling programs, academic advisement, mentoring, and other methods of enhancing student understanding and acceptance of the procedures and steps necessary to accomplish personal and career goals are necessary.

For financial aid, the major issues are the acquisition, training, and deployment of staff to provide a one-stop, total-package financial planning service for community college students. In many respects, the financial aid office is the heart of the institution, since for a majority of current personnel, it demystifies the requirements and procedures of ever changing federal, state, and local programs of financial assistance for higher education. Often, the first level of demystification lies in translating the argot of financial aid into terms that students with limited ability to comprehend written English can understand. The second level relates to developing an understanding in students of the requirements of high-level money management and personal finance under circumstances frequently involving no exchange of the real dollars to which they are accustomed. The third level relates to developing among financial aid staff members an accurate and working familiarity with the copious rules and regulations of federal, state, and city public assistance programs that directly affect students' eligibility for higher education assistance and students' ability to matriculate in postsecondary institutions in the context of families, jobs, housing, and other personal matters.

A most important issue to be faced in the area of financial aid is directly related to the backgrounds that nontraditional students bring to community colleges and to the expectations that community colleges can realistically set for their progress. The issue is this: If a steadily increasing number of entering students require remediation, and if under present circumstances it is unreasonable to assume that years of underachievement can be overturned in one or two semesters, especially when a student lacks proficiency in the English language, then it becomes essential to put in place financial aid programs that will allow students to complete their programs of study in community colleges in six or eight regular semesters rather than in the traditional four. The state of New York recognized this problem and recently inaugurated a special tuition assistance program, which augments the tuition assistance program by providing two additional semesters of financial aid for students who require significant remediation.

The second major area of policy, management, and programmatic changes to flow from the open-admissions policy involves curriculum revision. As students enroll in community colleges in response to changes in the community — increasing unemployment, curtailment of public assistance programs, rising standards for general and technical skills in entry-level jobs, and so forth — a majority of colleges are experiencing a growing imbalance between student demand for career and technical programs and demand for liberal arts programs. While student demand for career-oriented courses is understandable, the imbalance inherent in this preference affects the entire college community, threatening the future of liberal arts faculty and raising questions about the ability of the college to graduate students who are not only trained in a skill area but who are also prepared for social responsibilities in a democratic society. The broader issue raised is what constitutes quality in community college education from the perspective of changing community needs and expectations. Many community colleges are experimenting with solutions or responses to this question by pairing courses, by establishing mandatory general education requirements regardless of career specialization, by instituting core curriculums, and by strengthening transfer programs and related support services, among other strategies.

Although the community colleges remain in a growth posture throughout the United States, on many campuses it is the continuing education divisions that are offering flexible programmatic response to community needs. Free of the established strictures of academia but having direct access to a talented and well-trained pool of academicians and career training specialists, these divisions are in a position to give the broadest possible meaning to the community college goal of community service. Certificate programs and special-interest courses for adult learners are becoming the bread and butter of continuing education divisions. As their missions are broadened to include outreach to assist communities in economic development, they will become more extensively involved in in-plant training and basic skills improvement in cooperative ventures with unions and other organizations representing workers on the job, with corporate management in devising and implementing retraining programs for management personnel, and with state and city agencies in the development of short-term employment and business development programs. It is not unreasonable to speculate that in the not too distant future continuing education programs on community college campuses will represent microcosms of the community colleges themselves.

Implications for Leadership

While there is general consensus on the routine responsibilities of the community college leader—board and community relations, academic and institutional leadership, planning and budgeting, and, most important, communication with students and other public constituencies—the elements of leadership required for community colleges in the mid 1980s and beyond add to these traditional elements an important new dimension that might best be described as the social or societal visionary. Presidents must sift through available data—television news reports; census data; employment and training trends in industry; shifts in federal and state funding patterns; board, faculty, and staff priorities and concerns; trends in enrollment projections and student career goals; dialogue with other presidents and colleagues; elementary and secondary education graduation and dropout rates; industry relocation efforts; new housing starts; and more—in order to come forward with a plan, a set of goals, an interpretation of myriad circumstances and likelihoods, a vision of what tomorrow will bring, and a vision of how best to prepare for it.

In this dimension, leadership involves analysis and interpretation of a massive, ever changing data base to develop a sensible point of view about the benefits that can be derived from redirection of resources within the institution. It requires an appetite for information of all sorts from all quarters and a mental capacity to digest and translate both the information and its utility inside and outside the institution. It also requires a mental facility to interact with myriad constituencies both pragmatically and philosophically. In the process of relating to numerous publics, the community college leader, as the symbol of his or her institution, gives clear signals of the institution's viability, visibility, vigor, currency, utility, and purposefulness. The extent to which he or she couples a facile command of broad-ranging information with an interpretation of its current and future relevance to the institution and the community plays a significant role in the public's perception and evaluation of the institution. In short, the leader confirms and maintains public perception of and confidence in the institution while at the same time serving as a catalyst for change in the community.

Leaders play a significant role in validating and legitimating the institution. In relating to board, advisory committees, students, faculty, employers, regulatory agencies, legislators, parents, community organizations, professional associations, business and industry leaders, support staff, and others, the leader uses the aura and power of executive office to interpret the benefits derived from interaction with the institution's resources and establishes these benefits as worthwhile contributions to individual and community goals.

Leadership in community colleges extends beyond effective and orderly planning in administering the institution. The resources available — personnel, buildings, equipment, and time — are essentially useless without an organizing and galvanizing visionary at the center. The leader, not the manager, is the galvanizing force for change in a period of economic and social dislocation experienced by individuals and groups in the community.

Reference

Naisbitt, J. *Megatrends.* New York: Warner Books, 1982.

Joshua L. Smith is president of the Borough of Manhattan Community College in New York, New York.

*Economic and political developments have caused community
college presidents to devote more time to external constituencies,
such as the legislature and business, and to form new alliances
among business, government, and education. The community
that community colleges serve is expanding.*

New Relationships with Government, Business, and Industry

John N. Terrey

When the Truman commission issued its historic report in 1947 (President's Commission on Higher Education, 1948), the word *community* became part of the title of two-year or junior colleges. The change was not merely cosmetic. This visionary report perceived a new, active role that placed community colleges at the center of external activities by serving community needs in a multitude of ways. As population shifts, economic fluctuations, political upheavals, and social changes change the community, the college changes. Hence, the efforts of colleges to serve the community can prove frustrating.

That relationships with external organizations are changing is one of the few certainties in community college education. Rather than defining the dynamics of change, it may be more appropriate to illustrate change by describing the relationships of community college leaders in Washington state with external agencies. There is one caveat: There is great disparity among community colleges and among state structures for community colleges. However, the trends facing leaders are quite similar.

R. L. Alfred, P. A. Elsner, R. J. LeCroy, N. Armes (Eds.). *Emerging Roles for Community College Leaders.*
New Directions for Community Colleges, no. 46. San Francisco: Jossey-Bass, June 1984.

The Washington State Community College System

A brief profile of the Washington community college system provides the necessary perspective. Following two years of economic woes, the state's financial condition appears to be stabilizing. However, the journey through financial chaos has had an impact on community colleges. First, it resulted in drastic dollar cutbacks, which reduced the number of students who could be served. For example, in 1980 the system served 104,000 full-time-equivalent students. Two years later, that number had declined to 82,110. The decline was the direct result of budget cuts, not of a decline in the demand for services. Second, the region's economic problems caused leaders to direct their attention to economic development and economic recovery, especially as these involved high technology, and to request assistance from community colleges.

Those students were served by twenty-seven colleges in twenty-three districts. Academic program enrollment is 53 percent of the total enrollment. State funds provide 91 percent of the operating budget, which means that the legislature is the primary external constituency. There is no local tax base. For the 1983–84 biennium, the state appropriation is $434,634,000 for operations. Tuition receipts are collected locally, but they are transferred to the state's general fund, where they are commingled with other general tax receipts. Against this political reality for community college education in Washington state, there are three main external groups with whom institutional leaders must relate: government agencies, the private sector, and educational providers.

Relationships with Government Agencies

State Legislature. With over 90 percent of institutional operating funds coming from the state's general fund through legislative appropriations, legislative activities are a top priority. The legislature also sets tuition, establishes salary increase percentages, and reaches into virtually every phase of operation; for example, local trustees are confirmed by the senate. Obviously, control of the community college has been shifting to the state level.

While decisions about the funding and operations of colleges are made at the state capitol, the typical legislator bases his or her understanding of the system on his or her understanding of a particular local college. If the legislator has a good understanding and appreciation of the local college, he or she usually understands and appreciates the system. Thus, individual legislators are a major external constituency for community colleges. To work with members of the legislature, two elements are required: a structure for legislative relations and presidential leadership. Presidents must understand the legislative process and the politically motivated behavior of legislators.

Legislative relations are becoming increasingly important for community college administration. Twenty years ago, legislative staffs were small, and they generally operated only during the session. Today, staffs are large, specialized, and largely full-time. The higher education committees of both houses have full-time staffs. Staff not only arrange hearings during the session but also organize interim studies, which usually include meetings and hearings. Likewise, the ways and means committees have a person on their staff who specializes in higher education. Contacts with these people are critically important. Making these contacts is a continuous task.

The Executive Branch. The governor plays a key role in the life of community colleges in Washington state. First, he appoints the members of the twenty-three local boards—each board has five members, who serve five-year terms—as well as the eight members of the state board, who serve four-year terms. Second, the governor prepares and submits to the legislature the biennial budget for the operation of state government, including the community colleges. The community college budget is developed in close cooperation with the governor's budget office. Thus, a working relationship with the Office of Financial Management is a subset of the working relationship with the governor. While some of the concerns are of a policy nature, a great deal of the work centers on details, such as the price of processing a library book or the student-teacher ratio. Competence is the basis for mutual respect in this relationship.

In recent years, governors have assigned specific responsibility for liaison with education to a staff person. The governor's education liaison can be a very important influence on the community college system. Presidents must understand and appreciate the delicate relationship of the governor's education liaison to the legislature, the community college system office, and individual colleges. In some cases, contact is almost on a daily basis; in other cases, there is contact only when there is a crisis.

The Legal System. The state's attorney general is the legal adviser to the state board and to the twenty-three local boards of trustees. Our society has become litigious. Presently, the Washington state community college system is spending $484,709 for attorney general fees to cover the period from July 1, 1983 to June 30, 1985. The attorney general currently has thirty-six cases pending in some stage of litigation. In addition, the attorney general prepares formal opinions on request. These opinions do not have the standing of law, but they are exceedingly important. In property transactions, contracts, and legal interpretations, the attorney general is a prime asset.

The Federal Level. Perhaps the greatest change affecting community colleges from the federal level over the past twenty years has been the growth of student financial aid. Today, student financial aid, especially the federally supported programs, is an essential element of college attendance for many students. Because tuition was low, financial aid was slow to become a major factor in the lives of community college presidents. Today, every president anxiously tracks congressional activities related to financial aid. It is big business.

For community colleges, vocational education is equally important. With about 45 percent of their enrollment in the vocational area, legislation and rules from the federal level are important. Approximately $5 million to support community college vocational efforts comes into the system annually from the federal level. Thus, college leaders must maintain congressional and agency contacts. They must also maintain contacts with the American Vocational Association and the American Association of Community and Junior Colleges. Vocational education is a critically important issue at the moment because the Vocational Educational Act is up for reauthorization.

Both student financial aid and vocational education operate in a political environment. The ten members of the congressional delegation in Washington state are assigned to a college president as their contact. When an issue arises that requires a contact with the congressional delegation, the college president becomes diplomat and politician. Contacts are usually restricted to members of the key committees considering a piece of legislation. Congressman Carl Perkins and his committee hold the fate of vocational education in their hands in the House, and a member of the Washington state delegation is a member of that committee; he receives numerous contacts on vocational education.

The entire federal structure—Congress, agencies, and associations—is an important external constituency. Influencing this structure is more important now than it was ten years ago.

Relationships with the Private Sector

Of all the external forces that community college leaders now face, relationships with business and industry aimed at economic development and recovery have become the most forceful. Ten years ago, these efforts demanded very little of a president's time. Today, as much as one third of a president's time can be taken up by these efforts. Consider, for example, the array of agency relationships and reponsibilities that fall within the purview of community college leaders in Washington state: The Commission for Vocational Education is the state agency designated to receive federal funds and manage the Vocational Education Act. State and federal legislation has changed its role in recent months to include management of a $3.5 million state-sponsored job skills program and the federally sponsored Job Partnership Training Act that becomes effective on October 1. The main objective of the Commission for Vocational Education has shifted to coordination of state and federal programs for the training of prospective employees to fill new jobs created by new or expanding industries. The Job Training Coordinating Council is appointed by the governor to designate service delivery areas that contain private industry councils (PICs). Many colleges are represented on local PICs, and presidential involvement is much greater than it was under the Comprehensive Employment Training Act. The High-Technology Coordinating Board was established by the legislature to direct the operations of a state-sponsored High-Technology Training Program. A sum of $3.5 million has been allocated to establish up to four demonstration training centers within the community college system. Community colleges will become an active partner with industry in high-technology training. The Governor's Committee on High-Technology Training and Advancement is appointed by the governor to review the state of high technology and to recommend needed improvements. A product of the committee has been a closer working relationship between business and community colleges.

It is difficult to overstate the significance of the relationship now being forged between business and industry and community colleges as the state struggles with the important issues of economic development and economic recovery. In the past, there were occasional meetings between the two groups. Each meeting tended to be a first meeting, and there was never a second meeting. As a consequence, there were no outcomes. The severe economic recession that hit the state in 1981 gave a sense of urgency to previous hit-and-miss efforts. The Northwest had been supplying 48 percent of the lumber used in the domestic market. By 1981, that figure had dropped to 28 percent. Unemployment in the state exceeded 13 percent. In some areas, especially in the lumber-producing areas, unemployment exceeded 20 percent. The aerospace industry was weak. Agriculture was soft. Necessity, the mother of innovation, closed the gap between business and education.

They discovered common bonds and set out to establish a constructive and effective working relationship through joint participation on economic development councils, chambers of commerce, and industry councils.

As industry and education have worked together, community college leaders have learned from business and improved their management practices. Two concepts that originated in the industrial sector and that are now being applied in the college setting are strategic planning and quality circles. Both industry and education have read *Theory Z: How American Business Can Meet Japanese Challenge,* by William Ouchi. From Ouchi's book, the concept of quality circles has been singled out for additional development as a means of fostering participation in campus decisions. Strategic planning needed a translator before it could be applied to the colleges. Steiner (1979) appealed to the business leader but not to his collegiate counterpart. Keller (1983) translated the concept into the college environment.

One of the unintended consequences of such reading is that it has provided leaders with a new sense of kinship. Misunderstanding and mutual distrust have tended to disappear, and a new base of commonality has been established. Leaders from both sectors are seeking new ways of doing old tasks. They concur with Cleveland (1972, p. 89), who wrote: "The future executive will be brainy, low-key, collegial, optimistic, and one thing more—he will positively enjoy complexity and constant change."

Discussions between the business and industry complex and community college leaders need to deepen. Vocationally oriented training may not be the real need. In the forthcoming information society, the change in the labor force is not very revolutionary. Over the next ten years, the Bureau of Labor Statistics forecasts a greater demand for janitors than for computer workers and a greater demand for health-related occupations than for either janitors or computer workers. There is a need for 600,000 new secretaries. Office automation has changed the secretary's world, but the transition from the electric typewriter to the word processor can be completed by a competent secretary in a week at most. Etzioni (1983) argues that students need psychic preparation for the discipline required for learning.

If change is to be a way of life, then community colleges must prepare people to think analytically and reason logically. Yet, we are putting the emphasis on narrow job skills that are destined for rapid obsolescence. This is fair neither to the individual nor to the employer.

Relationships with Educational Providers

As an institution, education is becoming increasingly complex. *A Nation at Risk* (National Commission on Excellence in Education,

1983) is a call to action on education that has made education a campaign issue for the 1984 election. Other groups, such as the College Entrance Examination Board, the Twentieth Century Fund, and the Education Commission of the States, have also issued reports. These developments have brought a new urgency to the continuing problems of articulation. The Washington state legislature has created a temporary committee to review all education. Membership includes a cross section of the state. It is a safe conclusion that the legislature is not content with the structure and operation of education. If it were, it would not have appointed a special committee to examine the structure of education.

Relationships between sectors have not changed so much as activities have increased. High school-college relations have seen a decided increase in activity, which has involved virtually every group within the education family — school directors, superintendents, college presidents, and trustees.

Conclusion

The constituencies with which a community college president must work are changing. More are off campus. While this is good in many respects, it has some potential dangers. The central activity is still education. One must be careful not to lose one's effectiveness with internal constituencies while improving one's effectiveness with external constituencies. In every solution, there is a problem.

The center for decision making has not shifted. Although the tight economy and increased legislative staff have increased the tempo of legislative activities, the key decision center is still at the local level. State-level activity tends to condition the environment, but it has not usurped the local decision process. In the community college system, there is a pragmatic reason for maintaining strong local bases. Legislative support is based on local issues.

Tomorrow's community college leaders must be able to merge the local concerns of business and industry, citizen groups, elementary and secondary education, and political officials with the statewide interests of the legislative and executive branches of government. They will need to clarify their thinking about the institution's roles and autonomy as a partner with public- and private-sector organizations in multiple programs. Most important, they will need to identify and address important questions about the cost-benefits of community college education for specific external constituencies. What training, narrow skill, or ability to learn is most helpful to industry in the long run? What types of cooperative programs for remedial adult education should be developed with elementary and secondary school systems? Until these questions are answered, community college presidents will manage, but they will not lead.

References

Cleveland, H. *The Future Executive.* New York: Harper & Row, 1972.

College Entrance Examination Board. *Academic Preparation for College.* New York: College Entrance Examination Board, 1983.

Education Commission of the States. *Report and Recommendation of the National Task Force on Education for Economic Growth.* Education Commission of the States, 1983.

Etzioni, A. *An Immodest Agenda.* New York: McGraw-Hill, 1983.

Keller, G. *Academic Strategy.* Baltimore: Johns Hopkins University Press, 1983.

National Commission on Excellence in Education. *A Nation at Risk.* Washington, D.C.: U.S. Government Printing Office, 1983.

Ouchi, W. G. *Theory Z: How American Business Can Meet The Japanese Challenge.* Reading, Mass.: Addison-Wesley, 1981.

President's Commission on Higher Education. *Higher Education for American Democracy: A Report of the President's Commission on Higher Education.* New York: Harper and Brothers, 1948.

Steiner, G. *Strategic Planning.* New York: Free Press, 1979.

Twentieth Century Fund. *Report of the Twentieth Century Fund Task Force on Federal Elementary and Secondary Education Policy.* New York: Twentieth Century Fund, 1983.

John N. Terrey is executive director of the State Board for Community College Education in Washington State.

Analysis of technological change and its implications for human resource development is an important task for community college administrators. This chapter reviews future changes in technology, their impact on faculty and staff, and the implications of changing technology for leadership development in the decade ahead.

Leadership and Technological Innovation

Ronald W. Bush
W. Clark Ames

Community colleges are being placed on the defensive as providers of postsecondary education in an era of multiple delivery systems. They are being pressed to document and defend their role in society, their mission, their curriculum, their right to legislative appropriations, their definition of the associate degree, and in some cases their very existence. The best defense is a good offense. Community college leaders will need to formulate an effective offense if they are to address two major obstacles that lie ahead: technology and human resource development. These two challenges need to be addressed together, because they will be inseparably intertwined as colleges allocate personnel to operational and strategic management functions. If proactive planning is an essential dimension of leadership, then analysis of technological change and its implications for human resource development is an important task for community college administrators. This chapter reviews future changes in technology, the impact of these changes on faculty and staff in community colleges, and the implications of changing technology for leadership development in the decade ahead.

R. L. Alfred, P. A. Elsner, R. J. LeCroy, N. Armes (Eds.). *Emerging Roles for Community College Leaders.*
New Directions for Community Colleges, no. 46. San Francisco: Jossey-Bass, June 1984.

Technological Assumptions

Those who believed that the hand-held calculator would be the supreme application of technology in the classroom proved short-sighted. Yet, those who project that all learning will take place in the "electronic cottage" by the 1990s are headed toward disappointment. The future lies somewhere in between. We know that the technological world is changing rapidly. The time required to develop and introduce increasingly sophisticated technologies has shrunk from a period of years to a period of months. The hardware of high technology in the form of satellites, fiber optics, computers, lasers, and robotics is becoming less expensive with each new advance. Stationary satellites, once a billion-dollar experiment, are now within the financial reach of individual community colleges. Fiber optic cables, which carry thousands of communications on a strand the size of a human hair, are being put into place by the long-distance telephone companies. Community colleges may be able to use advanced technology to link multicampus districts or to allow colleges to share resources. Computers have gone from a multimillion dollar investment primarily for large organizations to a relatively inexpensive item well within the financial reach of individual faculty members. Robotics and laser technology have important implications for complex organizations. In addition to its amazing medical applications, the laser is being used in such applications as high-speed printers that quietly produce twelve pages of text per minute. Robotics are being introduced in industrial and office settings. In the not too distant future, we can expect to see robots delivering the campus mail and vacuuming the carpets. These futuristic technologies are still quite expensive, but we can assume that they will follow the developmental path of other technologies.

The software of high technology has a dramatic impact on the capabilities of these new technologies. Just as a new video cartridge changes the game on a video screen, new software packages change a personal computer into a word processor, a calculator, an electronic spread sheet, or a terminal that can access a computer network. For a knowledgeable or adventurous faculty member, the possibilities are endless.

It is important for community college leaders to recognize the full impact of this technological revolution. Although the specific nature of technological change is an issue of concern, it is not the issue of consequence. The fact that change will occur, that it will be less expensive than other alternatives, and that community colleges must be prepared to use the emerging technology is the paramount issue.

The technolgical revolution will soon require instructional programs to incorporate technological advances in order to make students competitive in the job market. Technological advances will become pervasive in the operation of administrative offices and classrooms. Faculty and staff must be prepared to use these technologies. Strategies must be developed, and dollars must be made available to make this change possible.

Technology, in particular communications technology, will have an organizational side effect beyond its direct application to administrative operations. Instantaneous communication capabilities through teleconferencing and electronic mail will encourage faculty and staff to expect up-to-date information on organizational issues and a broader voice in organizational policy making. Technological advances will be used to enhance organizational effectiveness. By maintaining a defensive posture and holding the line on the introduction of new technologies, community colleges could allow uninformed staff to dictate organizational direction—potentially with catastrophic consequences. The more productive strategy is to take the offensive by developing flexibility that enables the organization to respond quickly to changing technologies.

Organizational Assumptions

The cost of the new technological resources will have some impact on college budgets. However, the costs are miniscule in comparison to the expenditures for human resources. Over 80 percent of the typical community college budget is allocated for human resources, and over 50 percent of the total college budget is allocated for faculty. The average lifetime cost of a tenured faculty member exceeds $1 million. Yet, over the years community colleges have routinely hired faculty and granted tenure.

By way of contrast, consider the procedures used to evaluate the acquisition and use of technology. On most community college campuses, the acquisition of a million-dollar computer is preceded by months of study and hairsplitting scrutiny. Organizational requirements are examined. The equipment is carefully reviewed to make sure that it will be cost-effective and low maintenance and that it will continue to meet institutional needs a decade or more into the future. A service contract is executed to make sure that the equipment remains up-to-date and operational. College administrators have been much less thoughtful with million-dollar investments in faculty and staff. Human investment also needs to be cost-effective and low-maintenance and to meet institutional needs a decade or more into the future. The equivalent of a service contract will need to be provided to ensure that these investments remain up-to-date and operational, that they are made with an eye toward technological developments, and that they are made within the context of a management philosophy that considers the institution's human resources to be its major resource.

Development of human resources in the context of changing technology will require careful thought and considerable imagination if community colleges are to respond effectively to changes in postsecondary education. In particular, three major areas require attention — the institutional environment, funding sources, and human resource development. These are familiar concerns. However, leaders will need to view them very differently in the future.

Institutional Environment. For most community colleges, new technology in the form of communications systems and expanded access to data bases will increase the pressure on central administration to share information. If the new communications technologies were used effectively, they could reverse adverse effects of earlier growth periods — such as the bureaucratization of the decision-making process, the detachment of faculty and administrators, and central control over information — and make full participation in management possible for faculty and staff. This development will force leaders to face some difficult choices. For example, leaders can choose defensively to control the amount of information that they share with different constituents in the college. Or — in our opinion the more viable position — they can take the initiative in using the new communications technologies to bring faculty and staff into the central information network. The second road is perilous, but it will allow leaders to take the offensive.

Employee groups will need to become sophisticated in their understanding of the budgetary, programmatic, and political environments in which the college operates if they are permitted to have full access to the central information network. Whatever the current structure of formal and informal relationships between faculty and administrators, new relationships will need to be forged that emphasize frank and open discussion about the implications of information for long- and short-term college development. Faculty and staff must also be brought into the development and implementation of policies and programs that affect not only compensation but careers, professional growth opportunities, and institutional direction. Employee-driven program development and implementation have time and again proved to be the most effective means of moving an organization forward rapidly and on course. However, this process can only succeed in an institutional environment marked by trust and the open sharing of information.

Funding Sources. Over the past decade, the willingness of governmental agencies at the federal, state, and local levels to fund community college enterprises has declined, and private sources of funds have been increasingly strained. Reduction of budgets for supplies and maintenance, many colleges have found, will not balance the budget when dollars are declining dramatically. What this means for community colleges is that educational leaders in the years ahead will need to become masters at using effectively the 80 percent of their budgets allocated to human resources. When this expenditure category is combined with effective use of technology, it points to new sources of funds that can increase institutional flexibility and enable the institutions to respond effectively to a rapidly changing environment.

Human resource programs need to demonstrate flexibility. A quick mental review of faculty and staff who have been at our colleges for a decade or more will bring to mind a number of burnouts. Early and phased retirement programs are one option that can promote flexibility. Many institutions have found that programs of this type — when designed and implemented by employees — can reap substantial benefits for both the employees and the institution. For employees, it provides a career option that can be used for actual retirement or as a springboard to another career. For the institution, it provides substantial dollar savings and a pool of available cash that can be used to redirect curricular emphasis.

A second career option to promote flexibility is the leave of absence. Without such a safety valve, many burned out and frustrated faculty and staff members are forced by economics to remain in their positions until they retire. By allowing employees to take one, two, or even three years of leave, the institution shares substantial benefits with the individual. The individual has time to rest and recuperate, to try out alternative careers, or to retool for new disciplines or job opportunities within the institution. The institution benefits through increased financial and programmatic flexibility and improved ability to make rapid shifts in response to changing technologies.

A third option, which is more a cost-containment measure than a means of freeing internal funds, is to develop a flexible benefits plan. If such a program is developed and monitored by employees, the cost of employee benefits can decrease. The flexible or cafeteria benefits program places the responsibility for selection of a variety of options on employees — both in the design of the benefits options and in the monitoring of costs. Before the advent of computerized personnel and payroll programs, it was not practical to give employees a wide selection of benefit options. However, computerization of records makes the administration of such programs increasingly possible. As a means of holding the line on costs, flexible benefits will become an increasingly important aspect of the human capital funding for community colleges.

Human Resource Development. In developing the human resources needed to respond to technological changes, leaders will need to examine—in concert with faculty and staff—the markets to which response is needed and the skills required of faculty and staff. A changing work force will require training oriented toward the rapid acquisition of new technological skills. There is a popular but false assumption that advanced technology requires advanced skills in order to be used. Experience has shown that the opposite is true. Community colleges are likely to find that they will constantly be retraining the same work force to use a different technology.

Currency in technology as well as the educational delivery process will become the paramount qualification for new faculty. Often, it will mean up-to-the-minute, hands-on experience in the field. Many instructors may come from the ranks of business and industry on a split contract. This need for currency may also mean that an instructor's tenure with the institution will last only as long as the need for retraining exists. Administrators will need to establish clear expectations for faculty and staff to remain current in their fields. This will mean that faculty and staff will need to be on the crest of the wave of advancing technology as both their disciplines and the delivery system change. It will also mean that administrators will need to provide employees with assistance to acquire whatever training they may need in order to remain abreast of the market.

Implications for Leadership

The rapid advance in technology in the years ahead, coupled with its dramatic impact on human resources, will require community college leaders to act in very different ways. Although it is difficult to predict the future shape of technology accurately, it is obvious that advances will occur. The institutions that will effectively meet the challenges ahead will be those that establish open systems for communication, that maintain flexibility in internal funding sources, and that create effective processes for human resource development.

The next generation of leaders will need to maintain constant vigilance over emerging trends in technology and the application of these trends to administration and instruction. Assessment systems will need to be developed both to identify new directions in technology and to gauge their impact on faculty and staff. The need to establish linkages with private-sector organizations heavily engaged in the application of technology will become critically important as a way of obtaining advanced information about technological change and its implications for instruction. Community college presidents and chancellors will need to work effectively with a wide variety of constituencies — business and industry officials, faculty, research scientists, public officials, secondary school teachers and counselors, university officials, and so forth — to ensure that decisions about technology are accurate, that they can readily be implemented by faculty and staff, and that they will yield cost-benefits for students. They will also need to realize that anger and frustration are going to be a problem for the 1980s as postsecondary education becomes more technological and computerized and as large numbers of faculty, staff, and potential students using dated methods to address complex problems are left behind.

Tomorrow's leaders will need to take risks in the types of decisions that they make, in their allocation and reallocation of resources to these decisions, and in the strategies that they use to motivate and develop staff to achieve important decision outcomes. In a period of changing technology, to adhere to the status quo is to guarantee failure. To attempt meaningful change through high-risk decisions is to guarantee success, even if the decision outcomes are marginal. The 1980s will belong to community college leaders who reject the status quo and take risks to ensure institutional development and progress in a bold new era.

Ronald W. Bush and W. Clark Ames are associated with the Maricopa County Community College District in Phoenix, Arizona.

PART 3.

Developing Community College
Leaders for Tomorrow

*Changing entrenched patterns of interaction among presidents
and trustees has great risks and great rewards. Acceptance
of personal responsibility for changing outdated patterns
of management is the president's task, while the task of the
trustee is acceptance of personal responsibility for selecting
a president who has the leadership capabilities to accomplish
this goal.*

Defining and Locating Effective Leaders

Margaret MacTavish

As community colleges have aged, the relationships among presidents, trustees, and faculty have come to follow unchanging patterns. Unyielding administrators require conformance with established policies and procedures, trustees take comfort in routine paper-shuffling board meetings, and entrenched faculty cling to conventional courses. Trustees who tolerate this condition, who do not demand leadership from presidents, sentence community colleges to an endless circle game. The absence of leadership guarantees organizational decay.

Changing entrenched patterns of interaction among presidents and trustees has great risks and great rewards. Acceptance of personal responsibility for changing outdated patterns of management through leadership is the president's task, while the task of the trustee is acceptance of personal responsibility for selecting a president who has the leadership qualities to accomplish this goal. This chapter outlines a contribution theory of leadership that specifies desirable characteristics in tomorrow's community college leaders. It describes changing environmental conditions that support this theory, and it concludes with a description of the presidential search process and needed changes if colleges are to recruit administrators who can provide positive leadership in the decade ahead.

R. L. Alfred, P. A. Elsner, R. J. LeCroy, N. Armes (Eds.). *Emerging Roles for Community College Leaders.*
New Directions for Community Colleges, no. 46. San Francisco: Jossey-Bass, June 1984.

Changing Environmental Conditions

Changing environmental conditions and the development of community colleges into mature institutions have changed the role of trustees. To some extent, changing conditions have also changed the benefits that individuals can expect to receive from service as a trustee. If trustees are to perform a meaningful role in the institution — that is, if they are to contribute to the development of the college in a period of change — locating and hiring presidents with desirable leader attributes will be important.

In the 1960s and early 1970s, trustees served as a resource for community college development. Whether elected or appointed, they knocked on doors to get petitions signed. They helped to design programs, and they made plans on kitchen tables. They stomped through the halls of legislatures seeking support. They pounded on the doors of the news media telling the community college story. Finally, when the fruits of their labors were ripe, they selected a president to carry out the college mission. The first generation of community college presidents enjoyed a very special relationship with their boards and with the staff whom they subsequently employed. Trustees were contributing to the success of the endeavor, and they knew it. Along with the president, they were writing the history of community colleges as they established new policies, approved new programs, and helped to pass bond issues that provided funds for construction.

As opportunities and new challenges were thrust on the institution during the 1970s, the demand for college programs and services grew every year. Faculty and administrators became impervious to failure. The organizational structure took shape, and legislative funding was not the pervasive issue that it is today. Presidents were creating, adding, building, and originating. They seldom found it necessary to eliminate, cut, substitute, diminish, reduce, or curtail. In short, they were not confronted with the need for change, and their tendency to use trustees as a resource diminished accordingly.

Today, presidents are faced with the need for drastic change directly related to the following conditions: changing demographics, the crisis in funding, increasing numbers of adult learners, competition from private education agencies and companies, changing national, state, and local economic conditions, technological challenges, the deterioration of college physical plant and equipment, aging staff, staff burnout, legislation and court decisions on comparable worth, the mid-life crisis of the community college movement, and pressure to reduce the scope of the institutional mission.

Community colleges have become unresponsive to these conditions because they do not use the full battery of their human resources — faculty, staff, administrators, and trustees — to address specific problems. Presidents are faced with the problems of dismantling and rebuilding troublesome internal systems within their colleges while at the same time addressing the conditions just listed. They also must deal with multiplying constituencies, which now include not only trustees, faculty, students, local elementary and secondary schools, and four-year institutions to which community college students transfer but also state and national legislative bodies, local business and industrial concerns, and special-interest groups within the service district, who all want more services and more programs from the college.

To administer our colleges in the future, leaders will have to subscribe to the tenets of contribution theory. Only leaders who use the full array of available resources through open communications and matching of personal values with institutional culture will be able to address complex problems within the framework posed by multiple constituencies. The array of available resources includes trustees. Trustees can contribute to institutional development by maintaining liaison with legislators and business contacts that can improve institutional resources, by applying their personal knowledge of the service region environment to the planning process, and by participating in community events that can improve institutional visibility. Trustees need to be involved. Like faculty and staff, they are a resource for institutional development — a resource that can be constructively used by presidents who possess leadership qualities that permit such use without causing anxiety or insecurity. The problem for trustees is how to find leaders who espouse the qualities of contribution theory.

Leadership as Contribution

Contribution theory postulates that leadership is a positive force needed to obtain maximum output from staff and trustees in discretionary activities essential for high levels of organizational performance. The basic tenet of the theory is that faculty, staff, and trustees have a strong desire to make a personal commitment that contributes value to the institution and to have that value recognized by peers, superiors, and subordinates. For presidents who desire to create an environment that maximizes individual contributions, contribution theory has five corollaries: First, know the historical, social, and economic undercurrents of the college, and accept personal responsibility for creating an environment in which faculty and staff possess the same knowledge. Second, use the organization structure to facilitate, not to hinder, progress toward goals. Third, communicate openly, and use both the formal and the informal communication networks. Fourth, identify ego traps, and avoid them. Fifth, know the culture and values of the college, and influence them positively.

Personal Responsibility for Institutional Mission. The president who is a leader spends the time necessary to define the mission and to disseminate information about the mission throughout the institution. In this regard, many presidents begin with development of short- and long-range plans for the organization, but two problems occur that sidetrack the process. First, they make these plans in a vacuum, involving very few staff. The result is an air of mystery. The majority of staff feel personally distanced from the plans, because they have not been involved in the process of making them and because they have not been told what is expected from them. Second, this kind of planning places the emphasis on the product — a volume, a brochure, a manual — that can be shown to staff, board, and community to prove that the college does indeed know where it is going. The result of this dissociation from the mission is the absence of personal commitment and personal responsibility for the institution. Multiply this dissociation by the number of staff, and it becomes obvious why institutional performance can suffer in the absence of leadership.

Facilitation of Progress Toward Goals. In a community college, the great majority of employees work in a framework in which multiple staff roles and multiple functions require cooperation among different units. Progress toward goals can be hindered when staff do not understand the nature of linkages between multiple units responsible for a single function. It is the responsibility of the president to make clear the mutually dependent relationships among staff in the organization. Leaders must expose the interconnectedness of staff roles if they are to take advantage of the collective talent and collective wisdom of the organization's members.

Open Communication Using Formal and Informal Networks. In every communication transaction that takes place in a community college, faculty and staff are determining how the communication affects them personally. Based on their perception of the meaning of the communication, they either accept or reject the message. They ask, "How will this affect me? Will I have to change my behavior as a result? Does it mean less work or more work for me? How does it affect my potential contribution to the college?" It is generally expected that presidents have acquired communication skills through formal education and experience. But have they?

Consider the sequence of events that occurs when a college president contemplates any change that affects staff. The president needs to disseminate information about the effects of the change throughout the organization. Even as this dissemination effort gets under way through formal channels, the informal network is already at work, and the nature and scope of the planned change are known within a short time. Presidents often do not take advantage of the quick flow of information through the informal network. They formalize the communication process, which results in attempts to keep the information confidential. As a result, a great deal of anxiety surrounds the flow of the information through the informal network, and the behavior of those who expect to be affected by the change becomes defensive.

Presidents who recognize that confidentiality is difficult to sustain over a long period of time, who acknowledge the usefulness of open communication, and who are prepared to use the informal network to disseminate information can do much to create a healthy environment for management. The president who communicates openly reaps the benefits of integrating the informal organization network into the formal organization structure. In a contributor environment, there are few valid reasons why access to information should not be free and open.

Identification and Avoidance of Ego Traps. One corollary of contribution theory — identify and avoid ego traps — will sound quite familiar to presidents who have been exposed to collective bargaining. In a collective bargaining environment, it often happens that a collective union ego and a collective management ego develop. A collective ego lives a larger-than-life existence. It exudes illusory power, and it operates as a protector of the individuals who give it life. All the reasons why unions can be good and productive forces in the college are valid until there is a rift between the collective management ego and the collective union ego. At that time, the organization in general and the president in particular encounter problems, especially if the president does not identify or recognize that he or she is dealing with a collective ego, not with individuals. The president who understands the nature of the collective ego and who can avoid ego traps is rare but desperately needed.

Consciousness of Institutional Culture and Positive Influence over Prevailing Values. The culture of a community college is defined by values reflected in the allocation of dollars in its operating budget and in the behavior of individuals. For example, if a president asserts that the college will be on the cutting edge of data-processing technology for administrative and instructional purposes, we expect to find this attitude prevailing throughout the institution. The state of the art in data-processing technology is completely revolutionized about every three years. Thus, if the college makes significant expenditures of funds but does not have state-of-the-art equipment, if operational activities have remained at the talking stage for three years or more, and if such comments as *If we had this computerized* or *If this were on the computer, we could* are heard, the president cannot support the assertion. The discrepancy between the president's words and college actions is a problem that needs to be addressed and resolved if the college is to move toward a contributor environment.

Searching for a Leader

The contribution theory issues many personal challenges to presidents and trustees. Trustees who are interested in institutional advancement are faced with the challenge of locating and selecting a president who bases leadership on his or her ability to implement the tenets of contribution theory.

Over the years, the presidential selection process has become a zero-sum game: The ad is placed, the applications and nominations come pouring in, the sort begins, and, in the final analysis, trustees select a president who fits stereotyped notions of what the community college president should be. They may parcel out various aspects of the process to headhunters or agencies. They may involve members of college staff, the community, students, alumni, politicians, or any number of other people. They may feel safety in numbers. The process may be technically impeccable, for it spreads responsibility around, but it does not often result in the hiring of a leader. No matter how many people are involved in the process, it is the trustees who are personally responsible for the decision. It is the trustees who either hire a leader for the college or who sentence the college to an interminable cycle of reactive or ineffective management.

Using the contribution theory, it is possible to define characteristics that the selection process should look for. The current practice is to establish easily measurable characteristics and to stop there. These measurable characteristics include: degrees, experience, personal and professional references, and achievements, honors, and awards. These factors can and should be used in the sorting process, which narrows the field of candidates, but they should not be used to select a leader. For example, the higher the degree and the more specific the major field, the easier the sorting process becomes. Further, a certain number of years at various administrative levels in a community college may virtually guarantee that candidates will have comprehensive knowledge of institutional management. However, it does not mean that candidates will be able to lead. Personal and professional references prove that some of those with whom an individual has been in contact express positive feelings about him or her, but that is all that they mean. Achievements, honors, and awards provide evidence that the individual has taken part in competitive activities, but they do not indicate that the individual possesses leadership qualities.

The desirable qualities in a leader are nonquantifiable and hard to find. These qualities include, without being limited to, the following: ego strength and inner confidence to be an equal contributor in achieving the college mission by accepting the assigned role of leader and facilitator; ability to create and disseminate a vision, to cast forth the seeds of ideas, and to cultivate their growth in others; ability to function as a change agent; ability to create consensus; and knowledge of how groups function and undertanding of the communication process.

The search for leaders with these characteristics begins with a letter to every college employee, full- and part-time, explaining the basic premise of the contribution theory. This letter should explain why their contribution is needed, wanted, and valued. It is likely that such an expression of caring about employees' personal responses guarantees a large number of responses, which should not be confidential but signed. The letter should ask six question:

- Without referring to a written statement and without discussing with your coworkers, your supervisor, or anyone else, will you write down what you believe is the mission and reason for being of this college?
- What, if anything, keeps you from making as great a contribution to the college as you want to make?
- What specific situations or ways of operating interfere with your doing your job?
- Do you have talents, skills, or abilities that you are not using now in your job but that you would like to be able to contribute to the college, even if this would be in another unit of the college?
- Can you tell us the kind of initiatives you would like to see the new president take that would make your job more interesting?
- Is there anything you would like to say about our upcoming search for the president?

All trustees should sign the letter. The text should thank employees for responding and make it clear that each response will be read and considered. The hard work begins when the trustees meet to study the responses. A person skilled in research techniques should be hired to summarize the results. Applicants who survive the first cut — that is, applicants who possess quantifiable characteristics of degrees, experience, references, and achievements — should be invited to answer a single question: How would you approach the job as president of this institution? The question should be accompanied by the summary of employee responses. Applicants' responses should be limited to six pages.

At this point, trustees should look for inner confidence, understanding of the role of leader and facilitator, ability to create a vision from the collective wisdom of staff, ability and interest in functioning as a change agent, ability and interest in gaining consensus, and understanding of individual and group dynamics. These characteristics are hard to measure. Nevertheless, consideration of them will narrow the field of candidates to a manageable number, who can be invited to campus for personal interviews. If the answers leave the number of qualified applicants still quite large, then a second question elaborating one or more items can be used.

The final steps in the selection process then become the personal interviews and on-campus visitations at the candidates' home institutions. At this point, it is appropriate to have the candidates exposed to as many elements of the college community as possible. The travel and lodging expenses for candidates are minimal, compared with the direct and hidden costs of an inappropriate choice. Candidates should be asked specific questions in the interviews. They also should be requested to cite specific examples of decisions that they have made, issues that they have resolved, and changes in organizational structure and management practices that they have initiated to improve the responsiveness of their institution to changing conditions. Candidates' answers should be evaluated in light of the tenets of contribution theory and employees' needs to determine whether the candidates possess suitable leadership characteristics.

The on-campus visitation at the current institution of employment for finalists is critical. The visiting team of trustees should develop their own visit agenda and allow two to four days to complete the agenda. They should talk with a broad range of campus and community constituencies as well as with elected officials, and they should talk with these informants about specifics. They should ask for examples, anecdotes, and illustrative incidents in which specific elements of contribution theory can be related to the candidate's leadership philosophy. They should plan to talk with different constituencies in different situations both on and off campus. Most important, they should select the types of persons with whom they talk. The candidates should not determine who is interviewed. If a candidate is a proven leader, this fact will be illustrated repeatedly by different individuals, in different settings, with different examples.

Every effort should be made during the campus visitation to isolate, document, and verify leadership characteristics desirable for effective performance in the presidency. Single-source testimony about leadership skills should not be accepted until it is cross-checked for accuracy against the observations of others. Only through exhaustive checking and cross-checking of information will trustees be able to determine that a given finalist possesses the characteristics desired in the president. Presidents who espouse leadership as contribution will be hard to find. However, a carefully developed and executed search process should result in the selection of a leader.

Margaret MacTavish is a trustee at Oakland Community College in Michigan and director of human resource management at Macomb Community College, also in Michigan.

A focus on women may provide some answers and insights into barriers that emerging forces in leadership must surmount in a male-dominated enterprise.

Tapping Neglected Leadership Sources

Judith S. Eaton

Community college education is being reshaped by the forces of limited financing, economic change, shifts in life-style and life expectations, and the demographics of our population. At the same time, a call is emerging for new leaders with new ideas to adapt our institutions to changing external forces. Where are these new leaders to come from? What is the present status of untapped resources — women and minorities — in leadership positions in community colleges? What are their prospects for the future? What actions might be taken to encourage a tradition of leadership among women and minorities in community colleges? A focus on women may provide some answers and insights into barriers that emerging forces in leadership must surmount in a male-dominated enterprise.

Women as Leaders

Women community college presidents and chancellors could barely fill a classroom. There are fifty female chief executive officers (CEOs) in public two-year colleges. There were eleven in 1975 (American Council on Education, 1982). While many hold the CEO designation, more than two thirds of these women report to another CEO (for

R. L. Alfred, P. A. Elsner, R. J. LeCroy, N. Armes (Eds.). *Emerging Roles for Community College Leaders.*
New Directions for Community Colleges, no. 46. San Francisco: Jossey-Bass, June 1984.

example, chancellor) rather than to a governing board. Twenty-four women head institutions with 3,000 students or fewer (American Council on Education, 1982). In 1982–83, the American Association of Community and Junior Colleges board had five women among its thirty-three members, and the Association of Community College Trustees board had ten women among its twenty-five directors. Relatively few community college women participate in the Project on the Status and Education of Women, the American Council of Education, or the American Association of Higher Education. Approximately 92,500 women are instructors or professors in community colleges, as compared with 142,000 men (AACJC, 1983). None of the emerging presidential and executive search consultant services is owned by women. There are two male administrators for every female administrator in the nation's community colleges.

Given this background, why should the leadership base of community colleges be expanded to include more women and minorities? The majority of students in community colleges are women. Community colleges serve more blacks and Hispanics than any other area of higher education. They have been urged to assume responsibility for improving the quality of education. This can take the form of encouraging long-term educational paths for women and minorities as well as of providing services to traditionally undereducated groups. Finally, enriching community college leadership by increasing the diversity of participation could increase the variety of perceptions and insights in the decision-making process and influence community colleges to improve their services to specific constituencies. Enlarging the leadership role of women and minorities increases the similarity between key decision makers and those affected by management decisions.

As women begin to move into positions of leadership, their patterns of behavior change. Behavioral patterns in the 1970s and 1980s can be characterized as follows:

1970s	*1980s*
• "Safe" pyramid: Women clustered at the bottom	• "Imperiled" pyramid: Women near the top
• Primarily an object of power	• Becoming a user of power
• "Superwoman" with multiple, often conflicting, roles	• Divorce and other forms of being alone
• No rules	• Emerging rules for dress, demeanor, sexuality
• Old queen bee: aloof, arrogant	• New queen bee: helpful yet successful

- Sexual target
- Not taken seriously

- Identified with women's liberation
- Emphasis on egalitarianism and sharing

- Living longer

- Nurturing of friendship and familiar values

- Sexual competitor
- Important competitor for big jobs, an alternative to cloning
- Situational minorities

- Emphasis on generation and other gaps and on networking
- Workaholic: high anxiety, high blood pressure
- Movement away from friends and closeness, nurturing of job values

Women continue to experience isolation, stress, and lack of power. They hold doubts about their legitimacy as managers and leaders. They need a model, a working profile of the woman independent of male models of management style. Donna Shavlik, director of the Office of Women in Higher Education for the American Council on Education (1983) and Bernice Sandler, executive director of the Project on the Status and Education of Women for the Association of American Colleges (1983) both acknowledge the leadership gains made by women in the last ten years, but they hasten to point out that women still face serious obstacles and problems. Shavlik sees significant growth at mid-level management but indicates that it is difficult to move into coveted CEO positions. Surprisingly, she states that men are more helpful to women in the community college movement than women are to women. Perhaps this is because men are more influential within the movement and thus more capable of helping women. Shavlik points out that there is still a need to encourage an image of women leaders with whom to identify. Systems are needed for working with women who are already in administration, and connections are needed between women in business and women in education. Women are not losing ground in these efforts, but they are temporarily stalled.

Sandler states that men are still not comfortable with women in leadership positions. Women are outside the prestige system in higher education, and they have been "backed off"—at least temporarily. Although change is occurring among mid-management personnel (and this includes women), the pressure to move women along is diminishing. Interestingly, Sandler sees men and women as viewing discrimination differently: Men see discrimination as overt, while women see it as silent, hidden, and insidious.

Preparing for Leadership

As community colleges advance toward the 1990s, women will mesh their unique history and struggle with the success and struggle of the community college movement. Women who use successful leadership styles for tomorrow will be aware of changing expectations for management and leadership. The organizational ethos of the 1950s and 1960s is increasingly viewed as inadequate and inappropriate for the 1980s. The shape of management is changing.

From	*To*
Acceptance of hierarchy: Position determines authority	Conflict about authority: Constituencies influence leaders
Benevolent despot	Cooperative, sharing leader
Assumption of continuing prosperity	Acknowledgement of financial uncertainty
Emphasis on work ethic	Concern about leisure
Charisma as a vehicle for control	Theory Z, systems management
Future perceived as secure: Trends continue, and planning is long-range	Future perceived as uncertain: Unique events predominate, and planning is strategic
Xerox machines, calculators, and Selectric IIs — the workplace supported by mechanical technology	Word processors and data base management systems — the workplace supported by electronic technology
Manufacturing economy, manual workers, and the superiority of professionals	Information and service economy, sunrise industries, and the new worker

Women who advance to CEO positions are likely to be individuals who can balance appropriate institutional needs with respect for individual professional performance. Those who strike a fresh bargain between what a college wants and needs and what faculty and administration want and need are likely to make headway. These developments, in addition to much-discussed changes in the community economic and social structure, will determine which management strengths have the greatest value in the 1980s. Women who become effective leaders will combine management and leadership traits in a variety of ways.

Trait	Avoid	Master
Effective and efficient use of time	Tyranny of urgency	Ambiguity
Tolerance	Quick aggravation	Effective dealings with people
Ability to motivate	Concentration on self-fulfillment	Focus on staff development
Strength of character	Indulgence in personal needs	Confidence in leadership instincts
Genuine leadership	Survivalism: living in the past, tinkering with the present, having no bold approach to the future	Risk taking
Participation in professional circles	Professional isolation	Preserving the inner you in a context of constant exposure
Ability to relax and enjoy events	Rigidity and narrowmindedness	Good judgment
Adjustment to stress	Overreaction to changing conditions	Development of alternatives

Empowering Emerging Leaders

Women who are presidents and trustees today are the potential national leaders of the community college movement tomorrow. Today's women in mid-management are tomorrow's presidents and chancellors. A great deal depends on how much emerging leaders want and on how high they place their expectations. Women faculty and administrators tend to tout minor successes as major victories. This can lead them to be satisfied with relative powerlessness. Women leaders need to become the norm rather than the exception — in their own eyes as well as in the eyes of men.

Professionals within the community college movement can pursue a variety of activities that will help to empower women as leaders. Administrators can develop goals around self-advancement and the advancement of women. They can hire qualified women for important jobs. They can institute cross training, internal sabbaticals, and other programs to advance qualified women to important jobs. They can share and encourage positive attitudes about women professionals with other men. They can become mentors and support mentors, and they can enhance networking. Faculty can stop doing too much work for too little recognition. They can become department chairs, they can support women for trustee positions, and they can support and encourage women in program development, service initiatives, and instructional changes. Finally, trustees can develop tactics that will empower women on boards in the community and in the state. They can hire a qualified woman for an important job, they can think about the impact of board behavior on women faculty and staff, they can work on negative attitudes in men and women board members, and they can become mentors.

Empowering women as leaders depends fundamentally on the establishment of familiarity with and about women. Lack of familiarity constitutes a major obstacle for success. This obstacle manifests itself both in male discomfort in working with women in unexpected roles and in women's difficulty in working with other women. The result is strain, awkwardness, and a breakdown in the convivial work bond so important to individuals in the workplace. Men and women need to learn new ways of sharing ideas and feelings; they need to develop new cues.

Empowering women also depends on the ability and willingness of women to incorporate strong leadership and management skills. While discussions of leadership sometimes contrast this complex of activity with management activity, community colleges need both kinds of skills. Considering individuals to be important, investing values in the job, having meaningful goals, maintaining a vision — all are frequently identified as parts of leadership. Efficient and effective use of resources, results, orderliness, and planning are expected qualities of management. Both complexes of activity are needed for leadership in community colleges.

If women can accept the challenge to integrate management and leadership skills, they will rise to positions of genuine leadership in the community college movement. Agendas will vary among institutions. In general, however, women will need to be prepared to deal with such issues as these: Course taking by working adults will take on new urgency in our changing economy, as mid-life unemployed workers in sunset industries seek retraining. Computers, television, and telephone lines will enrich institutional capacity, which will become other than campus-based and classroom-bound. As public support diminishes and as need for educational services increases, private support through institutional foundations will become more important. Vocational education may come to exceed two years. Academic skills will become increasingly important as vocational tools. Open admission will be joined by limited-entry programs. Education prescriptions for part-time students will be established, and admission will be limited to those whom community colleges can effectively serve. Finally, community colleges will join forces with school districts and universities to address issues of excellence in education.

The empowering of women means that they will need to have experience with the issues just outlined. They can attain this experience through work relationships with strong mentors, both male and female. Obstacles posed by unfamiliar work relationships, lack of familiarity with executive style, and academic traditions that preclude rapid progression in careers will need to be overcome. Although women may have to work hard in order to overcome obstacles, the present need for visionary leadership in community colleges gives them an opportunity to make major gains in acceptance, influence, and power.

References

American Association of Community and Junior Colleges. "AACJC Annual Report 1982." *Community and Junior Colleges Journal,* 1983, *53* (7), 30–31.

American Council on Education. *Women Chief Executive Officers in Colleges and Universities.* Washington, D.C.: Office of Women in Higher Education, American Council on Education, 1982.

Sandler, B. Personal communication, March 22, 1983.

Shavlik, D. Personal communication, April 4, 1983.

Judith S. Eaton is president of the Community College of Philadelphia in Philadelphia, Pennsylvania.

*Important and useful knowledge can be acquired through
academic training and therefore through graduate programs.
This chapter suggests ten areas for study that are vital for
leadership development in remodeled programs of graduate
education.*

Developing Leaders Through Graduate Education

Thomas W. Fryer, Jr.

It is appropriate to begin a chapter concerning the academic preparation
of persons to serve in positions of community college leadership by setting the matter in perspective. Some outstanding administrators have
had little if any formal preparation, and some ineffective administrators
have had outstanding academic preparation. Academic training can
develop potential and improve the performance and effectiveness of
persons who have it, but it cannot create potential.

Administration is a practical art. Even so, its practice is always
based on value assumptions and theoretical principles. Some practi-
tioners are not consciously aware that this is the case. In this chapter,
the term *administration* is used to mean the handling of routine matters
concerned with organization maintenance. It also involves critical
matters that contribute to or detract from the long-term viability and
overall effectiveness of the organization.

Dimensions of Graduate Education

Knowledge that is important and useful for college leaders can
be acquired through academic training and therefore through graduate

R. L. Alfred, P. A. Elsner, R. J. LeCroy, N. Armes (Eds.). *Emerging Roles for Community College Leaders.*
New Directions for Community Colleges, no. 46. San Francisco: Jossey-Bass, June 1984.

programs. That knowledge can be organized into ten key areas or dimensions of study. These dimensions are considered in this section.

The most important set of assumptions that any administrator holds has to do with his or her beliefs concerning the nature of human beings. Are people basically trustworthy or untrustworthy? Are they basically honest or dishonest? Are they fundamentally responsible or irresponsible? The sophisticated view asks, Under what conditions are human beings trustworthy or untrustworthy, honest or dishonest, responsible or irresponsible?

A community college is profoundly shaped by the explicit and implicit answers to these questions given by persons in positions of authority. Most graduate programs designed to prepare persons to serve in administrative posts do little to help administrators to identify and analyze the assumptions on which their actions are based. It is possible for persons to serve as competent administrators for a lifetime and never to become consciously aware of their basic beliefs and values. Nevertheless, value assumptions should be addressed explicitly, because the quality of any work force, including the quality of community college faculty and staff, depends on the quality of management. It is not likely that a highly motivated, creative work force will develop over time if there are not effective leaders to guide decisions. These leaders are sensitive to the conditions under which individuals perform most capably. Graduate preparation should address these matters as a first priority.

The second area of emphasis is closely related to the first. It involves both theoretical and practical work concerning human behavior in organizations and organizations as natural systems. This work should explore research data concerning positive human behavior, how to achieve it, and how to maintain it over time. As part of this work, the graduate student preparing for leadership should be required to set forth in writing his or her own "philosophy of people" and the value assumptions that underlie his or her behavior toward organizational participants.

Related to this area is the critical topic of accomplishing the work of the organization through group process. In today's complex, often large, educational organizations, few decisions are made by administrators in isolation. Almost all decisions are made during or after elaborate consultation. Often, the consultation process itself is the vehicle by which decisions are made. Future leaders need training in the effective use of groups as well as in the processes of group leadership and motivation. Enabling every participant in the group to bring his or her maximum intelligence to bear on the decision-making process is a challenging goal for any leader.

The fourth dimension of training emphasizes principles of effective personnel practice. Such principles should approach personnel issues from a comprehensive human resources perspective rather than from a procedural perspective, and it should contemplate an active rather than a passive work force. Six areas should be addressed: differences and similarities within and among constituent elements of the work force, such as faculty, classified staff, and administrators; listening skills; preparation of performance evaluation and appraisal documents; principles of collective bargaining; principles of affirmative action; and the range of personnel classification and salary systems. Effective techniques and forms of interaction among organizational participants should be identified, described, and practiced.

Principles of law and their application are the fifth area that the graduate training experience needs to emphasize. The approach here is not the traditional school law course that tends to recapitulate the history of major court cases. The emphasis should be on legal principles, including the concept of due process of law, as these principles are likely to operate in an institutional setting. Such a course should be devised with the active participation of seasoned attorneys who have served in the field as general counsels for community college districts.

Principles of financial management are the sixth important dimension of academic preparation. Such principles should not approach the topic so much from the perspective of recipes as from the conceptual perspective of developing an analytical understanding of where and how the organization derives its income and where and how the organization spends its money. Practical descriptions of risk management, energy conservation, and revenue diversification are important. Principles and techniques for the allocation of scarce resources should be stressed, and ways of improving efficiency and productivity in the educational enterprise without damaging the teaching and learning process also need some attention.

Principles of data-processing and information systems are the seventh area for graduate preparation. Information technology is an indispensable resource in the modern environment. It is also a major cost item in the complex organization. It is almost never used to the fullest extent, and most chief executive officers have the lingering fear that they could and should be achieving greater results for the dollars invested. A comprehensive on-line management information system is increasingly becoming a requirement for the large community colleges. The costs of such systems are enormous. Their design and development require tremendous concentrations of human and financial resources.

Eighth, the preparation of persons for positions of leadership should address the principles of planning. Historically, planning documents have been among the most-emphasized and least-used resources in the organization. Often, plans have been like the sidewalks that nobody uses, because everybody walks on the paths that appear to be shorter routes to the same places. Planning processes and planning results that are not integral to the way in which day-to-day decisions are made have a high probability of gathering dust on the planners' bookshelves. Actively involving faculty and staff in the process is vital to the development of plans that will affect future directions in positive ways, but wide participation often changes the nature and course of planning, because it makes planning less predictable, both in timing and in outcome, and because leadership must work hard to assure crisp definitions and clear work products. Thus, the preparation of leaders should include an assessment of a variety of planning techniques, especially those suited to turbulent and uncertain conditions.

Ninth, principles of research design and method, evaluation of evidence, and probability theory and statistical techniques are important aspects of preparation for effective leadership. It is doubtful that the typical statistics course provides the orientation that is required. The emphasis should be on principles and concepts rather than on recipes and techniques.

Last, programs to prepare community college leaders should provide a sense of the history of the community college movement and the evolution of the community college concept in the context of American postsecondary education. Professional administrators need to understand the concept of lay control of public education, and some introduction should be provided to the issue of working with governing boards. Programs should familiarize students with the bibliography and the critical thinking of others. They should provide a sense of the community college mission and substance—including students, curriculum, and educational processes—and they should provide at least an overview of American postsecondary education in the comparative context of other societies, both East and West. State and federal structures should be treated along with a practical approach to an all-important subject: the politics of education.

Desirable Leader Qualities

In addition to the ten dimensions of knowledge just outlined for graduate study and investigation, it is appropriate to suggest some qualities or characteristics of the effective leader that may be susceptible to development through academic training. Persons well prepared in all the areas mentioned in the preceding section would most probably be ineffective in leadership if they lacked many of the characteristics listed here. How such characteristics are to be cultivated, or even whether they can be cultivated, are difficult questions. It is not likely, however, that persons can serve as effective leaders over time unless they possess most of these qualities:

- Optimism, a positive orientation to life and people
- A well-developed sense of humor
- Above average intelligence, but not a dazzling I.Q. Too much intelligence may be as great a handicap as too little
- High tolerance for ambiguity and uncertainty and the capacity to hold open the decision-making process until a variety of alternatives have been explored
- Ambition, which may ultimately be no more than the ongoing desire to do one's job better or to make his or her organization more effective
- A vision of a better future and a sense of purpose and forward movement in the organization
- The psychological capacity to permit others to take credit for one's own ideas
- The emotional and professional courage to make difficult decisions, especially in personnel matters, which depart from the line of short-term resistance and point toward a more effective long-term future
- The capacity for surgical decisiveness when it is needed
- A positive orientation and a gut-level desire to say yes rather than no, coupled with the ability to say no when every fiber of one's being wants to say yes
- Common sense
- Good judgment
- The capacity to see complex reality as a whole
- Strong entrepreneurial orientation
- Capacity to get the job done, to work productively, to complete assignments on time with a high level of quality
- Verbal facility
- The ability to write
- The capacity to grow and profit from vicarious and intellectual experience
- The ability to acknowledge the stake that every constituency has in the enterprise and to provide legitimate opportunities for these constituencies to participate in the management and leadership of the organization

- Orientation to continuous personal and professional growth
- Some mileage on the machinery (nothing substitutes for experience)
- A balanced sense both of doing things right and of finding the right things to do
- The intellectual capacity both to disaggregate interrelated data and to synthesize disaggregated material
- A sense of the surrounding community and organizational context
- An appreciation of political process as a means for conflict resolution and accommodation
- An appreciation of compromise as a technique in problem resolution, balanced by a sense of those matters that ought not be compromised and by an unwillingness to compromise the future for short-term solutions
- A healthy sense of perspective about one's own importance and standing in the passage of time and the history of the human race.

This list of qualities, long as it seems, is incomplete. It is offered only to provide some sense of the form and texture that characterizes the role of leader and manager in a complex educational organization. There are many styles and approaches to management tasks. The same situation can be handled effectively in a variety of ways. There is always an important interaction among conditions, personalities, and history in a given situation, but it is important for the person who wants to become a leader to be impressed with a deep sense of the personal responsibility that derives from serving in a position of authority, however complicated the situation.

Conclusion

Producing the learning and the qualities that are desired in administrators requires a complex curriculum and educational strategy. Most existing courses in graduate-level programs will be wide of the mark. The ten dimensions of study suggested in the first section of this chapter are important in the preparation of administrators, but they do not all lend themselves to presentation in a typical semester- or quarter-length course format. Short, intensive course packages are probably more effective as vehicles for presenting the material. The typical graduate faculty in education may not be fully qualified either to develop or to present the material. Many of the desired skills require presentation from the perspective of other disciplines: psychology, sociology, business administration, and so forth. Able, effective, practicing administrators must be involved in preparation of the subject matter. Probably the most effective approach to the preparation of new leaders in today's era of limits in American postsecondary education is the pluralism that now characterizes the field.

That pluralism needs to be supplemented with a new type of program. One of the principal weaknesses of some existing university-based doctoral programs is that they require people to move through a prescribed sequence of activities that does not always meet their needs or remedy their individual deficiencies. By the time people enter doctoral programs, they vary widely in the extent to which they already possess the desired qualities or they have already learned the appropriate material. Inflexibility is a handicap to an effective training experience.

However, one of the principal strengths of the traditional doctoral program is that by its very magnitude and complexity it sets forth a challenge of significant proportions. Those who successfully complete the program have mastered a course that can build their confidence and help orient them to a world of difficult challenges. To the extent that traditional doctoral programs reduce their requirements and lower their standards, this virtue is eliminated.

Among existing nontraditional efforts, the Nova University doctoral program is important for making extensive practical use of first-rate professionals actively working in the field. Efforts within the profession itself, such as the Presidents' Academy of the American Association of Community and Junior Colleges and the Management Training Institute of the Association of California Community Colleges Administrators, have their place. Such programs as Harvard's Institute for Education Management also serve an important purpose.

An extremely exciting and potentially effective model lies in the development of a regional consortium of community colleges for the purpose of leadership development with a major research university at the consortium core. Universities can and should provide leadership for the organization of such consortia. The university's principal resource in such a venture is its faculty in the academic disciplines. An advisory group of leading community college professionals should assist in designing the program. Both short- and long-term training experiences should be developed cooperatively for potential administrators or for those who are already serving as administrators. The doctorate would be an appropriate degree awarded on completion of the longer and more comprehensive experiences. Well-designed administrative internships can be extremely valuable components of such programs. To the extent that consortium regions are relatively compact in size, administrator exchanges, internships, and other jointly planned experiences can have a highly positive effect.

Such an effort could be mounted in the university with one or at most two professional people based in the school of education if they drew extensively on universitywide resources. Considering the enormous need for training a new generation of leaders for community colleges and the lack of existing programs built on the principles and subject matter described here, grant funds should be available for the development of such programs.

Currently, a second generation of post–World War II leaders is serving in the top ranks of the nation's community colleges. This group replaced an earlier generation of practicing administrators who developed their skills during the decades of enormous growth and diversification. The great names of that golden era have given way to younger people, hundreds of whom were trained in university-based Kellogg Junior College Leadership Programs across the nation. Time passed, however, and the year 2000 approaches. Without conscious attention to state-of-the-art preparation of a third generation of leaders for America's 1,200 community colleges, the quality of leadership in these institutions may not match the complex challenges that will confront them.

Thomas W. Fryer, Jr., is chancellor of the Foothill-DeAnza Community College District in Los Altos Hills, California.

Leadership development is a process that must continue
beyond the experiences provided in graduate education. This
chapter examines the role that work experience plays in leader
preparation from the perspective of a unique program in the
Dallas Community College District.

Building Leadership Expertise Through On-the-Job Experience

R. Jan LeCroy

To become a leader, one must grow professionally. To remain a viable leader, one must continue to grow. Logically, then, leadership development is a process that must continue beyond the experiences provided in graduate education. The college environment must provide continuing learning experiences both for leaders in the making and for chief executives. The work environment can then become a laboratory for continued learning, whatever the previous, formal learning experiences have been.

Although it would seem logical that community college campuses would provide the best working environments for this kind of experiential preparation, that is not always the case. Community college faculty and staff working both to accomplish the open-door mandate and to provide a quality learning environment have found themselves caught up in the issues and problems of managing day-to-day work, a reality that has made it increasingly less possible for professionals to break free of tight schedules and to continue to learn or develop new insights. Community college leaders need to continue to refine their skills while at work if excellence is to be achieved.

The value of experience and continuing education in leader

R. L. Alfred, P. A. Elsner, R. J. LeCroy, N. Armes (Eds.). *Emerging Roles for Community College Leaders.*
New Directions for Community Colleges, no. 46. San Francisco: Jossey-Bass, June 1984.

development is not unique to community colleges. Kanter (1980), a professor of sociology at Yale University, speaks of all higher education as lacking developmental experiences for professionals. Even the best and the brightest leaders and potential leaders may come to feel stuck in academic settings. Analyzing the developmental patterns of adults, Levinson (1978) has pinpointed similar concerns. He sees academic settings as environments that frequently lack undergirding relationships to speed both professional and personal growth. Both authors stress how important it is for developmental needs to be met during a professional's career. Both offer professional development options that have value for community colleges and that the Dallas Community College District has developed.

This chapter examines the role played by experience in the preparation of leaders from the perspective of a unique program in the Dallas Community College District. It describes learning experiences that are important for emerging leaders, and it presents experiential principles that culminate in the cultivation of leadership skills. The chapter concludes with a discussion of mentoring relationships and of the critical importance of these relationships to leader development.

Leadership Development in the
Dallas Community College District

Through necessity and forethought, the Dallas Community College District has been able to develop an effective program for leadership development. Our basic approach can be summarized by amending the old chestnut Experience Is the Best Teacher to Experience Is the Most Pervasive Teacher. Perhaps other methods are more exciting, but stressing experience as teacher has proved a steady course to follow, and it has provided the conceptual backdrop for a sound professional development program. Ways have been found to provide experiences and professional relationships that are developmental in nature, that speed professional growth, and that culminate in leader preparation.

Practically speaking, when developmentally rich experiences and relationships are offered at the community college, certain obvious benefits occur. First, the development of leaders becomes a more cost-effective process. The bulk of cost can be absorbed by in-kind expenses. Leadership development through on-campus mentoring relationships is often an ad hoc process, informally arranged and voluntarily assumed at no monetary cost. Such initiatives are also time-efficient. The learning process develops close at hand.

Second, the experience as teacher approach is organic in design. The learning experiences that it offers are more likely to be integrated into the values of the organization. Recent research suggests that traditional staff development initiatives — workshops, retreats, conferences, short-term courses away from the college, even away from the work environment — tend not to be internalized. A professional who travels to another location, learns something new and stimulating, and returns to the campus to share the new knowledge is likely to run into difficulty if immediate implementation is the goal. To bring about successful change, a cluster of people sharing common experiences and relating to one another on a daily basis must own and then shepherd a new idea within the organization for an extended period of time. This reality is often frustrating to those who want the organization to grow in innovative ways, but it does stress the need for colleges to become laboratories for leadership development and the need for growth to be homegrown in design.

Leadership development through an experience-based program is an enlivening process. In describing the moving and the stuck, Kanter (1980) explains why enlivening occurs and why it is healthy to an organization. If emerging leaders believe that they are stuck, that there is no place to go within the organization, there is a strong likelihood that they will eventually become emotional dropouts on the job. Typically, they risk less. They may simply go through the motions, or pockets of discontent may develop. Women in particular have frequently experienced this sense of powerlessness in professional bureaucracies. And, since there are so many women of merit in the community college movement, the loss of their initiative and talent is staggering. However, if options are provided through experiences and relationships for leaders in the making, then the work becomes vital and forward-looking.

The Career Development and Renewal Program

In the Dallas Community College District, the task of leadership development is approached in two separate but complementary ways: The Career Development and Renewal Program (CDRP) offers a formal structure to promote organized learning experiences, and a mentoring network promotes strong professional relationships among staff. Developed in 1974, the Career Development and Renewal Program is intended to meet three primary goals: to offer renewal and career path training to staff, to create a resource bank of professionals as likely candidates for internal promotion, and to broaden and enhance understanding of the Dallas Community College District and of community college education in general.

The CDRP offers three types of learning experiences to participants. The first option is to propose and develop a special project. A professional working on such a project seeks out a special interest or concern and maps a course of study and reporting mechanism to shed light on the problem and offer potential solutions. The project assignments are structured in a number of ways. They can be accomplished over and above the staff member's regular job responsibilities, they can become part of those responsibilities for a specific period of time, they can be completed during a summer work period, or they can be accomplished during a partial or full release-time arrangement. In the past, special projects in the Dallas Community College District have dealt with a broad array of issues: student marketing, productivity, lifelong learning, liaison programs with high schools, four-day summer sessions, and quality-of-work-life initiatives.

The second option open to participants is to become an understudy. A professional so designated "shadows" another employee in the district whose work is of interest. An understudy may wish to learn more about a career path opportunity, to develop a better understanding of another work area that interacts with his or her own, to develop new skills that will be used in the current work assignment, or to compare the approach of his or her own work group with that of another unit. Since the understudy projects do not generally require staff replacements, cost is kept to a minimum. An understudy might typically spend one day a week observing the work of another professional. A division chair might wish to observe new computer applications developed by a district business officer. A counselor might observe a financial aid officer in an attempt to better understand and perhaps to clarify their complementary roles. A faculty member might work with an instructional development specialist involved in adapting mass media technologies to the classroom.

The third option for program participants is an internship. Often, the intern substitutes for someone on leave or serves as temporary replacement for a position that has not been filled. Usually, an intern replaces someone higher in rank. This creates a ripple effect within the district. A division chairperson may intern for a vice-president of instruction, who may intern with the president of a college. Then, as frequently happens, the division chairperson's position is filled for the semester by a faculty member. Although an internship usually requires a greater budget commitment than the other two options, it has been a highly successful method for generating creative energy within the organization. It is truly amazing what one learns from looking at the world of work from another point of view. Generally, the consensus among college faculty and staff has been that sufficient long-term benefit accrues through the interning process to make it a useful and cost-effective way of developing talent from within.

The initiative for being part of the CDRP comes from prospective participants, who volunteer. The program and its options are open to faculty, administrators, and noncontractual staff, who submit a formal application explaining the nature of the proposed activity and identifying in concrete ways what they hope to learn from the experience. Applicants submit their proposals in the early spring, and the proposals are reviewed by supervisors. Recommendations are then forwarded to the district office. The final selections, which are based on merit and quality, are made by the executive council. Generally, participants are notified of their selection by the end of the spring term and begin their work the next fall. As part of their involvement in the CDRP, they are expected to attend an orientation, several workshops, and special activities.

Approximately 150 professionals in the district have been involved in the CDRP, and about a third of the understudies or interns have assumed the positions that they explored as participants in the program. Four of our seven college presidents have participated in the program. Vice-presidents representing business affairs, educational affairs, and student development have participated in the program. A number of faculty have been involved in special projects and in various administrative assignments.

It is fair to say that programs of this type are easier to implement in large districts than in districts where there is lower enrollment and fewer staff. The Dallas Community College District contains seven colleges, two district sites, and literally hundreds of staff who can be moved within the organization. Using the jargon of innovation, we can describe it as an information-rich learning environment. It has growth potential and resources that offer a large number of options. Thus, it is more capable of institutionalizing a significant innovation than an information-poor environment would be. In that sense, as in the case of individuals, organizations that are rich in professional resources become richer. However, it is also fair to say that the district has valued professional growth, made it a priority, and taken the time to organize professional growth experiences into an ongoing, highly credible, and visible program designed to provide staff with the kinds of learning experiences that build leadership skills.

Examining principles that undergird CDRP training experiences shows why experience-based leadership development processes are effective. First, the program offers breadth of perspective. It offers a way of avoiding the tunnel vision that comes from unrelieved work at the same job. This is not to say that it is necessary to work at all the jobs in a college in order to become a leader in the work setting. Rather, the process is holographic. The freshness of the experience and the intensity of learning enables the professional to understand the whole environment coherently. A dozen internship experiences are probably not necessary for a leader in the making, but one good internship experience may be necessary for the emerging leader to formulate a broad vision of community college education.

The specific training provided through the CDRP is another valuable outcome. Corporate trainers occasionally decry educators for continuing to keep professional development activities one step removed from the practical learning of new skills. Perhaps because the European-modeled classrooms characteristic of community colleges have taught faculty and staff to learn about rather than to practice new processes, development opportunities have been structured as times when staff listen to experts, take notes, and discuss new ideas but fail to practice skills. The CDRP is a learning-by-doing operation.

Personal enrichment has been another desirable outcome of the program. Several dynamics are at work. It is invigorating to learn new ideas, to develop new skills, to find new relationships, and to view the institution from a different vantage point. At the same time, personal enrichment occurs when a participant learns that this new corner of the world is not to his or her liking. Too often, professionals are moved into roles for which they are ill suited. Unfortunately, a notion is circulating in community colleges that movement is good, promotion is to be devoutly desired, and professionals are to hunger for something more or different. This is simply not the case. Renewal for professionals through a CDRP-type experience may simply mean returning to a position and a work setting with a renewed sense of its suitability and responsibility. That is an outcome not only to be accepted but to be applauded.

The last positive outcome is organizational renewal. The CDRP experience as teacher model encourages flexibility and adaptability, two prime requisites for organizational health in the years ahead. An exciting new management theory developed by Hackman and Oldham (1980) suggests that the renewal of work—improving its quality and enjoyment—may depend on an organization's ability to redesign traditional jobs that may no longer be appropriate, that may be outdated, or that may no longer offer challenge. Organizations and work groups are much more likely to construct healthy work environments if they retain flexibility and adaptability as organizational traits. The face of work will be changing dramatically during the next two decades. Programs like the CDRP in the Dallas Community College District prepare staff for changes that inevitably will come.

Mentoring Relationships

From a personal standpoint, one form of the experience as teacher model has more to do with the development of leaders in community colleges than any other: The cultivation of mentoring relationships. The dynamics of a good mentoring relationship become a powerful tool in the development of leadership skills.

Levinson's (1978) research offers an overview of the mentoring relationship. The mentor, who is generally several years older and who possesses greater experience and seniority, acts as teacher, host, exemplar, and counsel for the young professional. He or she is willing to use personal influence to speed the young protege along the way. Levinson points out that one of the great paradoxes of human development is that we are required to make critical occupational choices before we have acquired the mature understanding to choose well. Thus, the mentor who has gleaned wisdom through years of experience helps to smooth the way. According to Levinson, the mentor is a transition figure and generally maintains a close relationship with the protege for five to seven years. The best mentors are middle-aged professionals who are in touch with their own youthful dreams. It is not wise for the mentoring relationship to continue indefinitely. However, when the mentoring period ends, there is a strong sense of loss. Levinson describes it as a loss of "resonance." Visceral, relational feedback is missing. This disconcerts both the mentor and the protege.

The mentoring relationship offers significant growth opportunities to both the protege and the mentor in a community college setting. The protege becomes better able to define skills. The protege is encouraged to develop skills and is frequently able to accomplish more than he or she dreamed possible. These opportunities come because of the quality of human interaction in the relationship. One of the most valuable gifts for emerging leaders in our colleges is feedback that can be trusted. Definition, encouragement, and empowerment come when an older and wiser person who is trusted takes an active part in personal development — pointing out the opportunities, identifying the pitfalls, making introductions, recounting organizational history, and softening the impact of awkward beginnings. Because community colleges are comparatively young organizations, prospective leaders must be able to gain credibility quickly. Trust and feedback become especially important in their development.

In relations of this type, the mentor gains considerably as well. He or she is prevented from being insulated. Community college leaders experience difficulty when they live in rarefied air and infrequently share new ideas or test their policies in professional exchange. Too often, experienced leaders develop a pragmatism that becomes cynicism. To be in touch again with the idealism that in all likelihood propelled the mentor toward a leadership role is a valuable outcome.

The complexity of the organizational structure in community colleges demands a sophistication of mentors that has far outstripped our cumulative understanding about relationships. In its simple form, a mentoring relationship is both professional and personal; it involves a comprehensive kind of personal interaction. Behavioral scientists have spent a great deal of time helping us to understand childhood and adolescence, but they offer much less help in understanding adult development, especially mid-life development. Certainly, if there is a dearth of mature, vital adults in our community colleges, there will be a dearth of mentors. It is already true that there are not enough able mentors to satisfy the needs of emerging leaders.

Community colleges need to remedy this problem through structured mentoring relationships. If they have good experiences in mentor relationships, proteges are likely to become mentor candidates themselves. Thus, when community colleges formally encourage mentoring, the likelihood that the number of such relationships will increase is great. At the same time, the visibility of emerging leaders in the work environment will increase dramatically.

References

Caswell, J. M. "Low Cost/High Value Staff Development Programs." *Community College Review,* 1983, *11* (1), 21–26.

Hackman, J. R., and Oldham, G. *Work Redesign.* Reading, Mass.: Addison-Wesley, 1980.

Kanter, R. M. "Quality of Work Life and Work Behavior in Academia." *National Forum,* 1980, *60* (4), 35–38.

Levinson, D. J. *The Seasons of a Man's Life.* New York: Ballantine Books, 1978.

R. Jan LeCroy is chancellor of the Dallas Community College District in Dallas, Texas.

*Material abstracted from recent additions to the Educational
Resources Information Center (ERIC) system provides
further information on community college leadership.*

Sources and Information:
The Community College President

Jim Palmer

No discussion of educational leadership can ignore the characteristics,
responsibilities, and impacts of the college president. Indeed, it is a
fundamental axiom that few educational or administrative initiatives
come to fruition without the support of the chief executive officer. As an
aid to researchers examining this pivotal leadership role, this conclud-
ing chapter reviews the latest ERIC literature on two-year college
presidents.

What Are the Characteristics of
Two-Year College Presidents?

Recognizing that insight into the backgrounds and educational
philosophies of two-year college presidents could improve our understanding of the colleges themselves, Young and others (1981) surveyed
the chief executive officers at 1,218 campuses, colleges, and districts
across the country. The survey solicited information about the educational and professional backgrounds of the presidents, their attitudes
and responsibilities, and changes in their attitudes and responsibilities
since becoming a college president. On a response rate of 61 percent,

R. L. Alfred, P. A. Elsner, R. J. LeCroy, N. Armes (Eds.). *Emerging Roles for Community College Leaders.*
New Directions for Community Colleges, no. 46. San Francisco: Jossey-Bass, June 1984.

the researchers found that 72.6 percent of their respondents held a doctorate, 84.2 percent had been employed in higher education for eleven years or more, and long-range, rather than immediate, administrative concerns had become more important since the respondents had assumed presidential responsibilities. The study also indicated that respondents were more likely to identify vocational education, rather than the transfer curriculum, as the top programmatic priority. Concomitantly, only 60 percent of the respondents felt that community college courses should be patterned after the courses offered at colleges to which most of their students transferred. The researchers concluded that since becoming presidents, the respondents' support for the university model of education had declined.

Since this study, which took place in 1980, no comprehensive national survey of two-year college presidents has been entered into the ERIC data base. For further information on the personal characteristics of presidents, the reader can consult American Association of Community and Junior Colleges (1982), a directory that presents brief biographical sketches of 887 chief executive officers at community colleges and college districts across the country.

What Remuneration and Benefits Do Presidents Receive?

The literature yields relatively little information on the salaries and benefits received by chief executive officers (CEOs). Nicholson (1981) conducted a study of the contract provisions, benefits, and compensation arrangements for two-year college presidents. This study determined that 72 percent of the CEOs had a contract and that the contract terms ranged from one to five years; 26 percent were for one year. While 40.5 percent of the contracts provided for annual review, only 2 percent of the contracts specified the CEO's basic duties. The mean salary of the CEOs in the study was $48,402.09, and the mean benefits earned by the CEOs amounted to $13,258. The most common benefit was a travel allowance (specified in 71 percent of the contracts), followed by life insurance (specified in 70 percent of the contracts), family tuition benefits (specified in 43 percent of the contracts), and housing allowances or the provision of a home (specified in 25 percent of the contracts). Nicholson also found a strong, positive correlation between institutional enrollment and the size of the salary.

Additional information on presidential remuneration at community colleges in California, Illinois, and Mississippi can be found in Garlock (1982), Kohl and others (1980), and Mississippi Gulf Coast Junior College (1980), respectively.

What Duties and Qualifications Do Presidents Have?

Much of the literature on two-year college presidents in ERIC focuses on the management priorities of presidents, on the qualifications needed to carry out presidential responsibilities, or both. This literature demonstrates the high degree to which declining resources are defining the leadership role of today's community college president.

In a nationwide survey of presidents at universities, two-year colleges, and four-year colleges, Patrick and Caruthers (1979) attempted to identify the presidents' priorities for planning and management improvements. The 300 public community college presidents who responded to the survey indicated that their top concerns (among the planning and administrative issues listed on the survey instrument) were, first, communicating institutional strengths to state legislatures, the public, students, parents, and state budget officials; second, providing for faculty renewal and vitality; third, improving procedures for the projection of enrollment; fourth, assessing institutional and program needs; and fifth, incorporating program review results into budgeting and program planning. These findings, the authors point out, are indicative of the no-growth environment of higher education. In such an environment, the president's job focuses on promoting the college among its constituencies, revitalizing aging faculty, maintaining enrollment, and evaluating college programs.

Jaap and Baker (1982) focused on the effects of collective bargaining on presidents' priorities. The authors surveyed 200 presidents, evenly distributed between colleges with collective bargaining and colleges without collective bargaining. Respondents were asked to rank administrative functions in terms of priority and time consumption. No significant differences were found between respondents at schools with collective bargaining and at schools without it. However, respondents in both groups ranked community relations, on the average, as the highest presidential role in terms of both priority and time consumed. Like the research conducted by Patrick and Caruthers (1979), this study underscores the importance of public relations in the president's effort to maintain institutional viability.

Other activities undertaken by the president to sustain the college include fund raising, service to the community, and morale building. Fisher (1982) argues that fiscal uncertainties will require presidents to pay more attention to the task of combining public affairs, publications programs, government relations, alumni relations, and other institutional offices in a centralized fund-raising effort. Vaughan (1982) notes that community college leaders who started their careers in the growth era of the 1950s and 1960s are susceptible to burnout in today's no-growth environment. Thus, Vaughan argues that one of the president's primary responsibilities is to prevent burnout—both his or her own and in faculty and staff. Finally, Stewart (1982) notes the responsibility of the president to lend his or her expertise to the community by taking on such tasks as managing a United Way campaign or preparing a budget for the local chamber of commerce. "Because all rights carry concomitant responsibilities," Stewart argues (p. 19), "the right that a college president has to lead the institution carries with it a responsibility to serve the community."

The responsibility of the president to maintain a good working relationship with the board of trustees has received considerable attention in the literature. Indeed, Marsee (1980) argues that the most important qualification of the president is his or her ability to work well with trustees. Thus, as King (1982) notes, the president must understand board operations, be sensitive to the time demands made on trustees, and project unconditional, positive regard for the board. Many articles on the relationship between president and board are contained in the issues of the *ACCT Trustee Quarterly (ACCT Trustee Quarterly. . .*, 1980; Hutchins, 1981, 1982). In addition, Hall (1981) discusses the overall relationship between president and board and examines their respective roles in college governance.

In light of the president's varied responsibilities, many authors point out the exceptional—almost superhuman—qualifications required of today's community college president. Griffin and Griffin (1981) list thirty-three requisites in the areas of personality traits, education and experience, management skills, and philosophical commitments to education. LeCroy and Shaw (1982) also list requisites, noting that the successful president must be skilled in long-range planning, program and personnel evaluation, collaborative decision making, and other areas. Nonetheless, contemporary observers are careful to note that fiscal and other problems will impede the progress of even the most highly talented president. As LeCroy and Shaw (p. 2) write, "No one of us, regardless of our skills, our preparation, our vision, or our charisma, will be able to alter the environment in which our colleges must function during the coming decades. But, we can play an important part in assuring that the community college remains a reasonably healthy institution in a changing context."

How Are Community College Presidents Evaluated?

Despite the importance of effective presidential leadership, relatively few authors focus on methods of evaluating the president. Henderson (1976) notes that presidential evaluation has several purposes: It stimulates productivity; it assesses the strengths and weaknesses both of the president and of the college; it provides a formal mechanism for the exchange of information between the board, the president, students, alumni, and other college constituencies; it assesses the effectiveness of the institution's response to college needs; it determines the extent to which the president has fulfilled the board's expectations of his or her promise and ability; and it measures the president's ability to continue to meet the evolving needs of the college. Thus, the evaluation of the president is closely intertwined with the board's ongoing assessment of the institution as a whole. Indeed, Henderson argues that the board's statements of institutional mission and management philosophy should be reflected in the criteria used to evaluate the president.

However, Seitz (1979) points out that the difficulty in developing objective evaluation criteria fosters continued use of subjective rating instruments that assess the president's popularity and personality traits rather than his or her contribution to the institution's progress and quality. He further argues that the unfairness of such evaluations is magnified when faculty and staff (who cannot assess the president's behind-the-scenes work) take a large part in the evaluation process. A proper evaluation, Seitz insists, is based on written standards of expectations that can be measured in terms of defined outcomes and that have been mutually agreed upon by the president and the board. "The accountability required in the objective method," Seitz argues (p. 15), "should be a welcome relief to those who are concerned about the inadequacies of trait scales, the vagaries of subordinate ratings, or the general lack of concern for measuring results factually."

While noting the importance of objectivity in evaluation, other authors maintain that subjective assessment can play at least some part in the evaluation process. For example, Henderson (1976, p. 5) concedes that "trustees often look for characteristics in their chief administrator which are important to them but not readily identifiable for evaluation purposes." These characteristics include integrity, judgment, and creativity. Nonetheless, Henderson stresses that the most effective and desirable evaluations are based on defined, measurable objectives.

What Does the Future Hold for Community College Presidents?

For many authors who discuss the future role of the community college president, that future is grim: Presidential leadership is stymied by a deteriorating economy, dwindling enrollments, bureaucratic red tape, and declining student skills. Stalcup and Thompson (1980) argue that the community college president faces an uncertain future, which is plagued with financial uncertainties, governance disputes, the competing interests of public interest groups, and collective bargaining struggles. These authors conclude that conditions will worsen for community colleges and their presidents, thereby increasing the challenges for creative leadership.

Besides external economic and demographic forces, future changes within the colleges themselves will further challenge presidential leadership. Eaton (1981) discusses these changes, which include growing professionalism among faculty and a concomitant deterioration of the college's hierarchical administrative organization and increased student demand for one-shot courses that meet immediate job training needs. Besides coping with budgetary pressures, then, presidents will have to use new approaches to participative management and develop new curricular structures that simultaneously maintain high academic standards and meet the educational preferences of students who stop-in and stop-out on an irregular basis.

In the face of these challenges, community college presidents will have to possess an extraordinary combination of management skills and leadership ability. Sullins (1981) argues that besides being outstanding managers, presidents must disentangle themselves from day-to-day administrative affairs in order to plan institutional responses to external changes. "In the rush to emulate our counterparts in business and industry," he writes (p. 28), "thousands of college leaders have become absorbed with the trappings of management tools and techniques and failed to recognize that successful managers in business and industry are also leaders." This concern is echoed by Carroll (1980, p. 3), who maintains that there is a strong temptation for administrators to become "passive managers of quantifiable activities." Master planning, accountability systems, and other management tools, she argues (p. 4), are a reaction to "the renewed interest in justification and accountability on the part of external agencies." Restricting the emphasis to management techniques "obscures and impedes the exercise of creative and dynamic leadership."

As the president's job becomes more difficult, he or she will be called on to do more than manage the college as an institution. He or she will have to study the implications of impending socioeconomic changes, determine institutional responses to these changes, and secure the commitment of the college community to implementation of these responses. The importance of planning in the president's leadership role is evidenced by the growing body of literature dealing with the probable impact of technological, demographic, and other changes on the community college. Authors speculating on the probable future of the community college include Breneman and Nelson (1981), Cross (1983), Gannon (1983), Koltai (1982), Nicholson and Keyser (1981), Simpson and Clowes (1981), and Wyman (1983).

References

ACCT Trustee Quarterly: Volume 4, Number 1–4, 1979–1980. Washington, D.C.: Association of Community College Trustees, 1980. 136 pp. (ED 196 463)

American Association of Community and Junior Colleges. *The Presidents and Chancellors.* Washington, D.C.: American Association of Community and Junior Colleges, 1982.

Breneman, D., and Nelson, S. "The Future of Community Colleges." *Change,* 1981, *13* (5), 17–25.

Carroll, C. M. "Educational Challenges of the 80's." Speech presented at the annual conference of the California Community and Junior College Association, Los Angeles, November 8–10, 1980. 17 pp. (ED 197 801)

Cross, K. P. "On Leadership and the Future of Community Colleges." Paper presented at the annual conference of the Association of California Community Colleges, San Diego, March 6–8, 1983. 22 pp. (ED 233 759)

Eaton, J. S. "Society 2000: Presidents and Prophecy." *Community and Junior College Journal,* 1981, *52* (1), 6–10.

Fisher, J. L. "The Two-Year College President and Institutional Advancement." In P. S. Bryant and J. A. Johnson (Eds.), *Advancing the Two-Year College.* New Directions for Institutional Advancement, no. 15. San Francisco: Jossey-Bass, 1982.

Gannon, P. J. "Future Outlook: 'World Class' Colleges." *Community and Junior College Journal,* 1983, *53* (7), 41–42.

Garlock, J. C. *Update Management Compensation. ACCCA Management Report, 1982-3/3.* n.p.: Association of California Community College Administrators, 1982. 32 pp. (ED 230 212)

Griffin, D. F., and Griffin, W. A., Jr. *An Ideal Community College President: A Position Description.* n.p., 1981. 8 pp. (ED 203 946)

Hall, R. A. *Challenge and Opportunity: The Board of Trustees, the President, and Their Relationship in Community College Governance.* Annandale, Va.: Association of Community College Trustees, 1981. 29 pp. (ED 201 362)

Henderson, L. G. *Some Recommended Guidelines for the Evaluation of a Community College President.* Tallahassee: Division of Community Colleges, Florida State Department of Education, 1976. 40 pp. (ED 180 534)

Hutchins, S. (Ed.). *ACCT Trustee Quarterly: Volume 5, Numbers 1–4, 1980–1982.* Annandale, Va.: Association of Community College Trustees, 1981. 132 pp. (ED 221 255)

Hutchins, S. (Ed.). *ACCT Trustee Quarterly: Volume 6, Numbers 1–4, 1981–1982.* Annandale, Va.: Association of Community College Trustees, 1982. 135 pp. (ED 223 296)

Jaap, W. M., and Baker, G. A. "The Impact of Collective Bargaining on the Administrative Functions and Roles of Community College Presidents." *Community/Junior College Quarterly of Research and Practice,* 1982, *6* (2), 157–166.

King, M. C. "Evaluation of the Boards of Trustees: A President's Perspective." Paper presented at the annual convention of the American Association of Community and Junior Colleges, St. Louis, Mo., April 1982. 11 pp. (ED 216 738)

Kohl, P. L., Wallhaus, P., and Lack, I. J. *Fall 1980 Salary Survey for the Illinois Public Community Colleges.* Springfield: Illinois Community College Board, 1980. 61 pp. (ED 214 548)

Koltai, L. *State of the District Address, 1982.* Los Angeles: Los Angeles Community College District, 1982. 18 pp. (ED 225 607)

LeCroy, J., and Shaw, R. "Community College Leaders for Tomorrow: Emerging Problems and Leadership Strategies to Avert Declining Resources." Paper presented at the annual convention of the American Association of Community and Junior Colleges, St. Louis, Mo., April 4–7, 1982. 15 pp. (ED 216 724)

Marsee, S. E. *The President's Relationship to the Board.* n.p., 1980. 8 pp. (ED 186 072)

Mississippi Gulf Coast Junior College. *Analysis of President's and Superintendent's Salaries.* Institutional Research Report No. 79/80–8. Perkinston: Mississippi Gulf Coast Junior College, 1980. 13 pp. (ED 192 835)

Nicholson, R. S. *Chief Executive Officers Contracts and Compensation, 1981: A Study of the Contract Provisions, Language, Benefits, and Compensation of Chief Executive Officers for the 1981 Year.* Washington, D.C.: American Association of Community and Junior Colleges, 1981. 63 pp. (ED 213 478; available in microfiche only)

Nicholson, R. S., and Keyser, J. S. *The Futurist Perspective: Implications for Community College Planning.* n.p., 1981. 15 pp. (ED 203 950)

Patrick, C., and Caruthers, J. K. *Management Priorities of College Presidents.* Boulder, Colo.: National Center for Higher Education Management Systems, 1979. 32 pp. (ED 212 210)

Seitz, J. E. "Evaluating Your President Objectively: A Message to Trustees." Paper presented at the national meeting of the Association of Community College Trustees, Detroit, 1979. 17 pp. (ED 191 524)

Simpson, J. R., and Clowes, D. A. (Eds.). *Virginia Community Colleges in the Eighties. [Proceedings of a Conference] (Blacksburg, Virginia, September 22–23, 1980).* Dublin, Va.: New River Community College and Blacksburg, Va.: Virginia Polytechnic Institute and State University, 1981. 102 pp. (ED 231 411)

Stalcup, R. J., and Thompson, W. A. *The Community College President: A Contemporary Janus.* n.p., 1980. 10 pp. (ED 187 402)

Stewart, B. F. "The President and Community Service." *Community and Junior College Journal,* 1982, *52* (5), 18–20.

Sullins, W. R. "Leadership in the 1980s." *Community and Junior College Journal,* 1981, *52* (2), 27–29.

Vaughan, G. B. "Burnout: Threat to Presidental Effectiveness." *Community and Junior College Journal,* 1982, *52* (5), 10–13.

Wyman, R. *Technology Is Ready — But Are We? Management's Challenge.* ACCCA Management Report, 1983–4/1. n.p.: Association of California Community College Administrators, 1983. 22 pp. (ED 235 852)

Young, R. B., Rue, R. N., Messersmith, L. E., and Gammell, W. "The Face in the Mirror." *Community and Junior College Journal,* 1981, *51 (5), 40–43.*

The full text of the documents for which an ED number is supplied can be ordered from the ERIC Document Reproduction Service (EDRS) in Arlington, Virginia, or viewed on microfiche at more than 750 libraries across the country. Readers should contact the ERIC Clearinghouse for Junior Colleges, 8118 Math-Sciences Building, University of California, Los Angeles, California 90024 for an EDRS order form and a list of the libraries that have ERIC microfiche collections. Items without an ED number are books or journal articles, and they are not available on microfiche.

Jim Palmer is user services librarian at the ERIC Clearinghouse for Junior Colleges, Los Angeles.

Index

A

Adaptation, and community colleges, 44–46

Admissions, and community change, 59–60

Alfred, R. L., 1–3, 7–19

American Association of Community and Junior Colleges, 68, 94, 99, 118, 123; Presidents' Academy of, 107

American Association of Higher Education, 94

American Council on Education, 93, 94, 99; National Identification Project of, 33; Office of Women in Higher Education of, 95

American Vocational Association, 68

Ames, W. C., 2, 73–79

Arizona State University, organizational studies at, 29, 30

Armenta, R., 31

Armes, N., 1–3

Association of American Colleges, 95

Association of California Community Colleges Administrators, Management Training Institute of, 107

Association of Community Colleges Trustees, 94

B

Baker, G. A., 119, 123

Basic Educational Opportunity Grants, 45

Birnbaum, R., 17–18, 19

Boards, local. *See* Trustees

Breneman, D. W., 21, 31, 123

Budgets, coalitions shaping, 9

Bush, R. W., 2, 73–79

C

California: minority students in, 57; presidential remuneration in, 118; state boards in, 47

Career Development and Renewal Program, 111–115

Carroll, C. M., 122, 123

Caruthers, J. K., 119, 124

Caswell, J. M., 116

Change: adaptation to, 44–46; assumptions about, 34–38; background on, 43–44; in communities, 55–63; in community colleges, 1; conclusion on 52–53; dimensions of, 43–53; in institutional environment, 46–49; and leadership, 1, 34–38, 41–79; in management, 59–62, 96; motivation for, 36–37; in operational approaches, 49–52; and systems technology, 51–52; technological, 73–79

Cleveland, H., 70, 72

Clowes, D. A., 123, 124

College Entrance Examination Board, 57, 71, 72

College without walls, as organizational alternative, 29–30

Commission for Vocational Education (Washington), 69

Communication, formal and informal networks for, 86–87

Community: analysis of change in, 55–63; background on, 55–56; external constituencies in, 65–72; and leadership implications, 62–63; and management requisites, 59–62; needs changing in, 56–59

Community colleges: adaptation in, 44–46; aging process for, 9–10, 13; change in, 1; history of, training in, 104; and rationality, 10; resource-dependent classification of, 30. *See also* Institutional environment

Comprehensive Employment Training Act, 69

Consortium, for leadership development, 107–108

Constituents: external, 65–72; and leadership, 50–51

Contribution theory: analysis of, 83–91; corollaries of, 85–88; and environmental conditions, 84–85; and searching for leaders, 88–91

Council of Great City Schools, 57